The Little Book of
REAL ESTATE
WISDOM

Garth Turner

KEY PORTER BOOKS

National Library of Canada Cataloguing in Publication

Turner, Garth
    The little book of real estate wisdom / Garth Turner.

Includes index.

ISBN 1-55263-518-X

    1. Real estate investment—Canada. I. Title.

HD316.T86 2002   332.63'24'0971   C2002-904189-9

THE CANADA COUNCIL | LE CONSEIL DES ARTS
FOR THE ARTS | DU CANADA
SINCE 1957 | DEPUIS 1957

ONTARIO ARTS COUNCIL
CONSEIL DES ARTS DE L'ONTARIO

The publisher gratefully acknowledges the support of the Canada Council for the Arts and the Ontario Arts Council for its publishing program.

We acknowledge the financial support of the Government of Canada through the Book Publishing Industry Development Program (BPIDP) for our publishing activities.

Key Porter Books Limited
70 The Esplanade
Toronto, Ontario
Canada M5E 1R2

www.keyporter.com

Brought to you in part by

Design: Peter Maher
Electronic formatting: Jean Lightfoot Peters

Printed and bound in Canada

02 03 04 05 06 5 4 3 2 1

Contents

Changing times, changing rules

The last time I wrote a book on real estate was more than half a decade ago. At that time the sexy money was going into mutual funds and stocks, not houses. Interest rates were far higher than they are today and the date September 11 meant just another day in autumn.

The technology bubble was just starting to inflate, and the media was full of positive news about Nortel, fibre optics and dot-com companies. Equity markets were rising fast with the Dow at the 8,000 mark and the TSE at 6,000—ironically, exactly where they would be again five years later, on the way down.

The biggest motivator for most investors was *greed*, driving billions of dollars in search of big, quick returns. The motivator as I write this is *fear*, which has driven that same money into cash and, especially, real estate.

In these intervening years it seems as if everything has changed. The technological revolution betrayed us. Corporate leaders lied to us. We saw the biggest bankruptcy in the world, Enron, followed an even bigger one, WorldCom. The promise of the stock market turned into the sting of decline. The forces of 9/11 attacked the very symbols of capitalism, and as a result we found ourselves taking off shoes and emptying purses to get aboard an aircraft flying from Calgary to Saskatoon. Interest rates plunged to historic lows, and suddenly you could rent $100,000 for less than $400 a month. In an instant one day, we all realized how cheap real estate had become. How affordable, and—in an era of terrorists and volatility—how predictable, and seemingly safe.

That resulted in a massive imbalance between supply and demand. Buyers lined up to shower offers on sellers. Bidding wars broke out in high demand neighbourhoods, and prices started to escalate wildly. At the height of it in April 2002, one agent in North Toronto shook his head as he told me about his clients who had bid $52,000 more than the asking price on a home, only to be beaten out by buyers even more desperate.

There were bidding wars in the cities and in cottage country. Homes in Victoria, Whistler, Edmonton, Toronto, Muskoka, Montreal, Halifax, and the South Shore were hot, hot, hot. For four of the first six months of 2002, there were more than 200,000 new houses under construction, on an annual basis—the best performance in a dozen years. In June, Toronto realtor Ellie Davis sold two homes in the north end for a total of more than $5 million. In that same market, 80% of all new housing being sold were condominiums, a situation that had last developed just before the great real estate crash of the late 1980s.

In Vancouver, in June of 2002, a West Side home sold for $6.6 million and the average home price jumped by 8% in a single month. Stephanie Corcoran of the Real Estate Board of Greater Vancouver commented, "It's reasonable to expect prices will increase." Financier Robert Campeau's old mansion on Toronto's Bridle Path went on the market at $8.9 million, more than $2.5 million over what it had sold for in July 1997, but $6 million less than the asking price back in 1994, when agents had to pay $100 every time they showed the property.

For the media, of course, real estate turned into an obsession, just as mutual funds had been five years earlier. There were lots of stories quoting credible sources like Canada Mortgage and Housing Corporation (CMHC) officials saying, "The bubble bursting is not a likely scenario."

In June of 2001, legendary developer and New York City billionaire Donald Trump came to Toronto to announce his partnership in a 60-storey condo/hotel in the heart of the financial core. The $800-a-square-foot project set a new standard for expensive real estate and boasted an $18-million penthouse. Thirteen months later, after the September attacks, the stock market meltdown, the descent of Nortel to almost penny-stock status, the accounting scandals, and the war in Afghanistan, came word Mr. Trump was pulling out.

So, what does this all mean?

Simply, that real estate is as changeable, volatile, and unpredictable as most other assets or commodities. Over the course of decades, just like the stock market, real estate gains in value—sometimes hugely. But over the course of a few months or a few years, the swings can be sickening. Those who misread the trends, who invest for short-term speculative gains, or who mistake a temporary fad for a fundamental shift, can go down in flames with the poor souls who thought 360networks, Global Crossing, or WorldCom were sure things.

Still, it is possible to create real wealth through real estate. Since we all need a place to live anyway, and since it is possible to leverage real estate through a mortgage—borrowing up to 95% of the purchase price—this is one of the easiest assets to own, especially when interest rates are low. Despite the 2001–2002 run-up in housing values, opportunity abounds for the serious investor, so long as you seek out properties that have a future.

Back in my 1997 book, I identified some of those properties: urban bungalows and homes in smaller communities clustered outside major cities; condos and age-proofed homes built for Baby Boomer seniors; cottage and recreational properties in the best locations; small apartment buildings; and, in niche markets, trophy homes.

Since then, I have largely been proven correct.

Bungalow prices have shot higher; satellite centres outside of Toronto and Calgary have seen massive development; condos have come to represent 80% of new home sales in Toronto, from 40% five years ago; demand has outstripped supply in cottage country; and lower mortgage rates have been translated directly into much larger homes.

THE BRIDLE PATH

Robert Campeau's estate

68 The Bridle Path (Lawrence Avenue East and Leslie Street)
Asking price: $8.9-million. Taxes: $61,890 (2001)

This stately 18-room French château, on more than four rolling acres in The Bridle Path, is a landmark estate, says listing agent Celine Joel.

Built by financier Robert Campeau in the mid-1980s, the mansion has everything from an elevator to a wine cellar, to an indoor pool and a bomb shelter. The latter consists of a living room, a dormitory and a two-piece bathroom, and is a self-sufficient space with its own generator.

The 314-by-961-foot grounds offer formal gardens, stone terraces, mature trees, fountains and a floodlit tennis court. Entry to the property is through wrought-iron gates and a circular driveway that leads to the nine-bedroom, 13-bathroom residence.

"Although the house was built in 1985, it looks like it's been there for hundreds of years," Joel says.

Guests enter the front foyer, which has a limestone floor and plaster crown mouldings, then pass through a grand foyer with a two-storey domed ceiling, cove lighting and a carved marble fireplace, before reaching the principal rooms.

"The grand salon" is a sunken room with a marble fireplace and five sets of French doors leading to the gardens and a patio. There's also a family room, a library-den and a pool room with cedar-lined walls and ceiling.

The 38-by-73-foot pool room has six double windows and a 22-by-44-foot chemical-free pool and whirlpool bath.

Cross-cut honey gold Travertine limestone flooring, washed maple cabinetry with pewter handles, and triple French doors to the patio are features of the kitchen. A butler's pantry off the kitchen has an elevator and access to the dining room. There's a service entrance with a door to the four-car garage, and a staircase to the upper and lower levels.

— Connie Adair
Listing Broker: Forest Hill Real Estate Inc.
(Celine Joel)

One of Canada's most fantastic houses, and a good indicator of shifting real estate values. Asking price, 1994: $15 million. Selling price, 1997: $6.17 million. Asking price, 2002: $8.9 million. *Source: The Globe and Mail*

Some of these trends will continue, due to the aging population and the inevitable, specialized demands that the largest crop of retirees in history will exert over the coming fifteen years. Demographics will have a huge impact on all of real estate, and the smart money will see that coming far in advance. I still believe that certain kinds of real estate, such as suburban, car-based, multi-bedroom homes, will inevitably tumble in value as birth rates decline. Other kinds, such as bungalows backing onto golf courses in cluster communities, will do very well. Still others that cater to fad, such as urban lofts, will prove to be sorry investments indeed.

This book seeks to put real estate in a proper, modern context in the first decade of the new millennium. Face it: Times have changed, and so should your investment strategies. Whether you are a seasoned veteran, or just yearning to acquire your first home, you must know what to buy, where to buy it, how to finance it, where to get proper help and advice, and how to avoid the pitfalls that have set so many people back.

We must remember that real estate investing in days like these is completely different than it was a generation ago. Today there is no built-in inflationary wave to push house values higher each year; the Canadian population is getting older, with 40% more seniors that just a few years ago, along with smaller families; and it is more important than ever to be thinking of resale value before you even make an offer to purchase.

The rules have changed. Learn them, live well, and prosper.

What really moves the markets?

Some people think the stock market and the real estate market move in different ways and for different reasons, with no real connection between them. But to think that way is a mistake. People who sour on stocks and mutual funds when the market is collapsing and rush into housing as an automatic safe haven had better watch out and understand the synergies between the two.

The last and greatest modern example of this was in the 1980s, when the stock market and the real estate market took a swan dive together. For those too young to remember, the equity markets died on October 19, 1987, when the Dow Jones Industrial Index lost a stunning 22% of its value in a single day. Since then, nothing has even come close. By way of comparison, the Dow gave up 13% in the first week of trading following the September 11 terrorist attack.

That 1987 plunge, as it turned out, was also the beginning of the end of a massive bull market in real estate which marked that entire decade. By 1989, sales activity in most major Canadian markets was petering out, just as the average home price was hitting its high point. Within eighteen months, the economy was in recession and real estate values, especially for condos, sunk dramatically. Thirteen years later, in the bull housing market of 2002, the average home price still sits below that of 1989.

So, what is the nature of the connection between stocks and houses? What does the relationship tell us of the future of housing values?

Both equities and real estate are moved by supply and demand. When more people want to buy a stock, like Nortel in 2000, then the price soars as demand chases supply. When more people want to bail out of their Nortel stock than there

Housing boom a salve to market weary

PETER REDMAN / NATIONAL POST

Despite numerous for-sale signs, housing supply in Canada is limited.

Continued from Page FP1

In the United States, money has been pouring into all kinds of real estate investments. Since January, investors have pushed US$2.41-billion into real estate mutual funds, compared with US$307-million in the same period the year before, according to AMG Data Services. The Bloomberg real estate index is hovering around a record high while house-building shares like Lennar Corp. are up 20% on a one-year basis.

In Canada, investors options are more limited, with publicly traded real estate stocks few and far be-

tween. However, Real Estate Investment Trusts (REITs) have been streaking to new heights. The CIBC World Markets Canadian REIT index closed June out at a 52-week high. The index was up 9.6% in the first six months of the year and nearly 18% in a year.

And, of course, home sales in both countries have been soaring. Sales of new homes in the United States surged 8.1% to more than one million for the first time in history in May. In Canada, home starts surged 10.1% in the same month to 203,200 at an annualized rate. Construction of single-detached homes hit their highest level since January, 1990.

The rush to housing has pushed

up home values, providing a welcome salve to consumers nursing stock market wounds. Indeed, the robust housing market has been cited as the primary reason U.S. consumers did not completely fall apart during the equity bear market and push the economy over the edge.

But underlying the new housing boom is a niggling fear that it might all end in tears like the late 1980s bust or the 2000 tech meltdown. Indeed, there have been two major themes coursing through financial markets in recent months: When will the stock market hit bottom and will the housing market crack?

The belief from almost all quarters is that while the real estate boom might cool off, it is in no danger of collapsing.

Considering what investors have been through in the past couple of years, that is a remarkably sanguine view and it all boils down to interest rates.

Jeff Rubin, chief economist at CIBC World Markets, who presciently predicted the 1989 Toronto real estate slump, said his call was based entirely on the view that John Crow, the Bank of Canada governor, would crank interest rates up to bring inflation under

---

After September 11, a massive shift of money took place, from stocks and mutual funds into real estate, attracting wall-to-wall media attention. Supply and demand moves both the stock market and the housing market, and in the 2001–2002 period, both were out of balance. *Source: The National Post*

are people who want to buy, the price falls. This fully explains why Nortel went from $120 to less than $2 in two years. It also explains why house prices soared in the late 1980s, as the Baby Boomer generation swamped the market; why they tanked in the early 1990s, as unemployment jumped higher; and why they boomed again in the early 2000s, as stock woes, terrorism, and accounting scandals drove millions of investors to look for safe alternatives to equities.

With stocks, supply and demand is dictated by corporate earnings, economic conditions, and the human emotions of greed and fear. With real estate, greed, fear, and demographics are important, but the greatest element is affordability. And affordability, in turn, is dictated by the combination of price and interest rates.

In the 1980s, the real estate boom ended for one simple reason: The average house became too expensive for the average family to buy it. That happened because house prices rose sharply during the boom, then interest rates also rose, making homes far less affordable. Suddenly people saw the real estate market as they viewed the stock market—as not giving good value.

Conversely, in the post–September 11 real estate boom of 2001–2002, investors were intensely motivated by the combination of relatively low prices and the cheapest mortgage rates in forty years, as the prime rate plunged to just 3.75%, and as all the major banks brought in "below prime" variable-rate mortgages. At one point in mid-2002, fully 70% of most borrowers had opted for the cheap mortgages that floated up and down with the prime rate. Affordability was the best it had been in more than a generation, just as the stock market started to sputter and move towards a collapse. So long as investors saw value in real estate, and not in stocks, then the money flowed.

As a result, there were multiple offers for all kinds of houses, rapidly rising prices, and a real estate mania. The average home price rose by ten times the inflation rate. Every month for more than a year, the Toronto Real Estate Board sold more houses

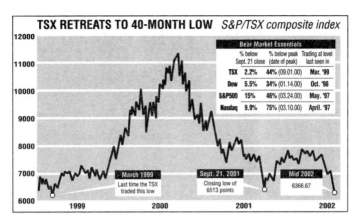

TSX RETREATS TO 40-MONTH LOW *S&P/TSX composite index*

	% below Sept. 21 close	% below peak (date of peak)	Trading at level last seen in
	Bear Market Essentials		
TSX	2.2%	44% (09.01.00)	Mar. '99
Dow	5.5%	34% (01.14.00)	Oct. '98
S&P500	15%	46% (03.24.00)	May. '97
Nasdaq	9.9%	75% (03.10.00)	April. '97

March 1999
Last time the TSX traded this low

Sept. 21, 2001
Closing low of 6513 points

Mid 2002
6366.67

Volatility on world stocks markets—thanks to a technology bubble followed by terrorism and accounting scandals—have many investors retreating to the perceived safety of real estate. *Source: Toronto Stock Exchange, Standard & Poors*

than ever before in history. New housing starts hit a twelve-year high. In May of 2002, for the first time ever, sales of new homes in the U.S. passed the million mark in a single month. That same month in Canada, the sales hit 203,000—twice as frenetic as the Americans on a per capita basis.

But all that activity came as interest rates started to edge higher and the economy grew stronger. The combination of higher mortgage payments and steeper house prices has meant an erosion in affordability. And that came precisely at the moment when a collapsing stock market meant everybody's RRSPs and mutual funds were shrinking fast. The conditions were gelling for change.

There are profound reasons to be a homeowner. You have to live somewhere. You can build up equity, and borrow against it. You can enjoy tax-free capital gains. You have a place to graft onto.

But those who try to time the real estate market usually end up just like those who try to time stocks. Understand why a house costs what it costs. If it costs too much, just think, "Nortel."

13

First, find out who's driving

Who's driving the market: the seller or the buyer? Your strategy as someone trying to get their hands on an affordable home, or trying to sell for as much as you can get, will vary tremendously depending on what kind of market is taking place.

Buying a home when the market is hot, prices are rising, and everybody is shopping can be a frustrating and expensive experience. But buying at a time when listings abound, prices are stagnant or dropping, and vendors are motivated can be a beautiful thing. Sometimes, many markets exist at the same time. Toronto could be hot, and Regina not. Bungalows could be going at an extreme premium to normal, while trophy homes change hands at far below replacement cost. There is often a major disconnection between rural and urban real estate, just as an entire province can be on sale after a change in government or a negative American trade ruling.

The point is, a market is a market, which means it is ever-changing and adapting every day to new conditions. This requires you to either do a lot of research on your own, or to work with a real estate agent who is part of that market and understands what strategies it requires. Personally, I would never attempt to buy or sell a property without an agent because chances are you will sell for less than you'd get with one, and pay more than you would without one (more on how to find the right agent later in the book).

What determines a seller's market or a buyer's market?

- **Supply and demand.** When supply swamps demand, the buyers call the shots. When there are more buyers than houses for sale, the shoe is on the other foot. The number of active listings changes daily, with sellers materializing when it is perceived that prices and demand are rising. For the last year or two, not enough new resales have come to market to satisfy the torrent of buyers—many of them stock market refugees—resulting in multiple offers and price escalation. It has also been a shot in the arm for the new housing industry, where buyers are largely spared from ruthless competition.

In a seller's market like the one that materialized after September 11, a common technique that developed was for a home to be listed, then held open for viewing for a day or two, with all offers accepted at a set time. The intent was to create an auction environment in which potential buyers would have to table their very best offer, or risk being eliminated. I was once caught in a situation like that, bidding for a townhouse against seven others. In order to win, my offer not only had to be tens of thousands of dollars above the asking price, but my agent had to deliver a massive down payment along with the offer, by way of a certified cheque—cash! My motivation was a looming travel schedule, otherwise I never would have entered into a fray like that!

Conversely, in a buyer's market, when there are tons of listings and a paucity of shoppers, things change dramatically. Desperate sellers are forced to give not only deep discounts on the appraised value of the real estate, but often have to take back mortgages at below-market rates in order to coax an offer. In terrible real estate markets, such as we had in the early 1990s, it is entirely possible to buy a property with no money down—by just assuming the existing financing. Supply and demand are crucial, but so are...

- **Mortgage rates.** Obviously, the lower the rate of interest on money you borrow, the more you can afford to borrow. The impact of rates on real estate is profound, and almost instantaneous.

THE VANCOUVER SUN

High-end homes in Vancouver's hot housing market are commanding multiple bids from buyers.

Consumer faith in economy, low rates drive latest boom

HOUSING
Continued from Page FP1

After four years on the sidelines, buyers are coming back, Ms. Corcoran says, motivated by record low interest rates and confidence that the economy will improve.

"It's really a simple issue of supply and demand," said Faye Lunday, a real estate agent at Dexter Associates. "In January, we had a situation where there was very little inventory and everybody was competing [for properties]. .

"A lot of [sellers] started jumping on the bandwagon but there are still a lot of people who want to get into the market."

The city does not have a lot of room to grow. The things that make it desirable as a place to live — the scenic Coastal Mountains on one side and the Pacific on the other — mean that useable land is in short supply.

"Compared to, say, Denver or

Calgary, where you can just keep pushing out it's more difficult to do here," says Jock Finlayson, executive vice-president of the Business Council of British Columbia.

Vancouver house prices started grabbing national headlines in the late 1980s and early 1990s. "A lot of that was fuelled by migrants from Asia, just before the repatriation of Hong Kong," said Cameron Muir, a senior market analyst at Canada Mortgage and Housing Corp. in Vancouver.

The big boom a decade ago featured dramatic price jumps. Otherwise modest bungalows in a desirable part of town were suddenly trading hands for unheard of prices, in some cases more than $1-million.

Not surprisingly, long-time residents who decided to take advantage and sell up — and many did — found themselves catapulted into the ranks of the comfortably well off.

What is unusual about the cur-

rent boom is that it is taking place at a time when the rest of British Columbia is suffering.

The provincial economy is mostly dependent on natural resources, which are in the dumper. The forest products industry — the biggest single component of gross domestic product — is struggling with punishing U.S. lumber duties. And mining is still on its back.

The frothy housing market in Vancouver points to the growing economic divide in the province — between the city and its thriving, diversified economy and pretty well everywhere else. "That means there's still a lot of people with well-paid, secure jobs," said Don Lawby, president of Century 21 Canada Ltd.

As long as interest rates stay low the market will stay hot, Mr. Lawby believes. "Here, as in most cities in Canada, there continues to be a really good demand and not a great amount of inventory.

"On the other hand," he said, "I don't think we are going to see some dramatic price increases [which we saw in the last boom]."

Financial Post
jgreenwood@van.nationalpost.com

It's a seller's market when consumer confidence soars and interest rates hit historic lows. In this kind of market, buyers have to be nimble and strategic to win the inevitable bidding war. *Source: National Post*

16

Following the terrorist attacks on New York and Washington in September 2001, the American central bank—the U.S. Federal Reserve—flooded the economy with liquidity to stave off any immediate financial collapse. That worked in the short-term, following which the Fed started to seriously lower the cost of borrowing to stem the possibility of a recession developing.

Interest rates were cut an unprecedented nineteen times, taking the prime to its lowest point in forty years. The Bank of Canada matched this, slicing its key rate, until the central bank rate touched an all-time low of 3.75%. At the same time, the country's major lenders were in a battle for market share, offering big discounts to posted mortgage rates, and also bringing in "below prime" variable-rate mortgages which provided Canadians with the cheapest money in the country's history. For example, at CIBC, the variable rate product offered a discount of 1.01% off the prime rate for most of the first year, then a quarter point off prime for the years following. It yielded an initial rate of slightly over 2.5%, and a giant leap in housing affordability.

Rates like this meant renters could suddenly become owners. More importantly, it meant buyers could demand more for their properties since they could borrow far more than in the past for the same monthly carrying charge.

In mid-2002, however, rates started to rise, with the Bank of Canada adding a quarter point on a regular basis, reflecting a rapidly growing economy and robust job growth despite ongoing stock market woes. The outlook now is for the prime to continue rising gradually through 2003 until it hits more than 6%. That is still relatively low by historic standards, and so long as the banks continue to offer below-prime money, the 70% of borrowers with variable loans should stick with them. The fly in the ointment, however, could be...

- **Consumer confidence**. Buying a house is a big deal for most people. Taking on a mortgage is daunting at the best of times, and usually impossible if someone thinks they may be in danger of losing a job.

  During most of the 1990s, people were negative about the economy because unemployment flared. The real estate market was in the doldrums. Then prospects brightened with the technology revolution of the late nineties, as the stock market soared and dot-coms abounded. That inflated the luxury housing market and especially the commercial real estate sector. In the early years of the new millennium, equities tumbled along with interest rates, but the Canadian economy vastly outperformed the American one, with 300,000 new jobs created in the first half of 2002. That was more jobs than in the rest of the G8 countries combined (United States, Britain, France, Germany, Japan, Italy, and Russia). As a result, consumer confidence—and real estate sales—bubbled.

Going forward, the major worry is that sustained weak stock markets will cause people to worry about their financial futures, their RRSPs and pension plans, both corporate and public. That could put a damper on real estate, or at least turn a seller's market into one that is a lot more balanced.

Longer term, inflation and interest rates should remain low, technology will bring down costs, and financial markets will improve—all positives for real estate. However, the aging population will change the nature and amount of housing on the market. Successful investors will be aware of all this and will stick a wet finger in the wind before doing anything.

Surviving in hot and cold markets

For sellers, it's quite simple: You will have to make concessions to sell when things are slow, and you can be demanding when the market is booming. In a buyer's market, the first thing to be conceded is price, followed by buyer incentives like cheap take-back financing and throwing in extra goodies, like a car or a boat. In a seller's market, you can always price your property a little below market value and, as mentioned above, create an auction environment by accepting offers only at a certain hour on a certain day.

As a seller, in a hot or cold market, the worst thing you can do is list the property above its market value. Your best shot at selling a house is within the first few days of listing it, and if the marketplace concludes that it's overpriced, the listing will grow stale fast—ignored by agents and their buyers. Ironically, the only real way to rekindle interest is to slash the asking price, often to below fair market value. It's the same old story—bulls survive, bears survive, and pigs get slaughtered.

For buyers, life is a lot more complicated, especially when the marketplace is buzzing with competition. Here are some eternal rules for achieving success in a hot market:

- **Pounce**. In boom markets, houses can sell in days—even hours. I have heard of homes that sell via cellphone from the agent's car, without the buyers even setting foot inside. This means you have to be ready to pounce in just a few hours, and mentally prepared to make an immediate—and likely unconditional—offer. This is not a time for deep reflection or indecision. It's cowboy capitalism at its best.

- **Be prepared**. To muster up a credible offer in a few hours means being pre-approved for a mortgage. This will eliminate the need to make your offer conditional upon financing—a condition which would give your paper the kiss of death in a multiple-bid environment. Being prepared also means having selected the lawyer you intend on using (you'll want him or her to quickly review your offer before presenting it) as well as a home inspector. Finally, you must have enough cash on hand to make the biggest possible down payment.

- **Be clean**. Any offer in a seller's market has to be clean of conditions. In fact, the best offer has no conditions whatsoever—certainly not conditional upon you being able to sell an existing residence. The seller doesn't care about that, so you must gamble that you can, in fact, sell for the price you want and not be left holding the mortgages on two properties. Can't stomach that? Then sell your home first, with a long closing, and go and buy a new home from a builder. The only little problem then is that the new home may not close before the old one does, meaning a few weeks or months in a motel.

- **Be flexible**. Since the seller is pretty much a god, he or she can demand what they want in terms of price and the closing date. Don't risk losing the home you want by being inflexible about closing. You can always arrange some bridge financing if you have a house of your own to sell, and if the two closing dates don't match up.

- **No inspection**. Used to be that no sane person made an offer that was not conditional upon getting a satisfactory home inspection (at the purchaser's expense). But times have changed. If you want to impress a seller, write in the home inspection clause, then scratch it out on the offer before it is presented. Your agent can then point to that as an indication you are seriously motivated and willing to take this risk. Unknown to the vendor, however, is the fact you took a home inspector along with you when you first viewed the property. No, that was not your brother with a flashlight.

- **Offer lots**. Offer as much money as you can, right off that top, taking your best shot. This might help you win—or even avoid—a bidding war. If your agent knows his or her stuff, you will have a good idea going in of what the market value of the property is, and what it might likely be worth in up to two years' time. That will guide your offering price, so long as you are prepared to live in that property for at least three to five years.

- **Set a limit**. Having said that, set a limit on the price you will pay, and stick to it. Take your available down payment, add in the maximum amount of the pre-approved mortgage, and use that as your gauge. If the money is insufficient to get the house you are targeting, then your real estate appetite needs an adjustment and you'd better look to a cheaper neighbourhood. Bidding wars are exciting, but often the "winners" can be the ones who will never see their investment fully returned to them.

- **Apply pressure**. The seller may be a deity, but you can pressure him or her into the kind of quick decisions they expect out of you. Make your clean, unconditional, rich, and generous offer to purchase valid for just a few hours—certainly no more than twenty-four. Each sign-back period, if there are any, should be shorter and shorter to get this piece of business done as quickly as possible.

- **Walk away** if things get out of control and the seller is delusional. Lots of houses come onto the market every day in

House prices leave buyers scrambling

First-time purchasers advised by veterans not to panic and to research opportunities

BY WALLACE IMMEN

In pursuit of their dream, many first-time home buyers in Toronto are finding that soaring real-estate prices are leading them to despair.

But veterans of the house hunt said it is possible to find the right home if you don't panic, and some predict that prices will level off as the warmer weather hits.

Domenic Capilongo calculated that $200,000 is the "magic number" that he and his wife could afford to escape a rented basement apartment in Etobicoke. But when the high-school teacher searched an Internet real-estate site, the number of homes available at that price came back zero.

"That was a shocker. We think we're making enough money, but wow," Mr. Capilongo said.

The kind of house he and his wife, Lynda Anthony, dream of, with space for a nursery for the family they want to start, would cost closer to $350,000, he said.

The average price of a resale house anywhere in the Toronto area reached $277,664, reflecting a rise of 11 per cent in the past year, according to figures released by the Toronto Real Estate Board this month. For a house in central Toronto, the average is $399,000.

"We've looked at shacks that you almost have to crawl into," Mr. Capilongo said; one place has only one bathroom, accessible through the kitchen.

The couple found an affordable option in Brampton but are continuing to search for a place closer to their jobs.

Janice Gladstone went through all the nightmares, but her advice is to keep trying. She is about to move into a house she and a partner bought in a corner of Riverdale for $300,000. "It helped that we were not desperate," said Ms. Gladstone, who teaches physics at Stephen Leacock High School in Toronto and was renting.

She had been looking at homes since last summer and had heard the stories of outrageous bidding wars, such as one on a detached house in Riverdale, listed for $360,000, that was bid up to $453,000.

"The areas that are peripheral to the hot part of Riverdale are a better investment," Ms. Gladstone said. The perfect opportunity finally came up in the neighbourhood near Jones Avenue and Danforth Avenue, and Ms. Gladstone she a strategy that allowed her to buy in without having to compete with other bidders.

In a hot market, buyers must be prepared to offer their best possible price in the cleanest possible offer. That means having mortgage preapproval and being creative about a home inspection. *Source: The Globe and Mail* most Canadian cities. Conditions can change rapidly. Don't feel pressured to accept too much compromise or to pay too much money. There are people today who bought under duress in 1989 and are still under water.

In a buyer's market, of course, everything is different and you are in complete and utter control of the home-buying process. So, enjoy.

- **Be tough**. Chances are, yours is the only offer the vendor is going to receive today, so it should be constructed to be entirely in your favour. Go after everything you want—the appliances, drapes, carpet, pool accessories, pieces of furniture, best closing date, small deposit, take-back financing, home inspection, and, of course, low price. The odds are almost certain the vendor will sign it back to you, outraged that you included his beagle and laptop, but you know that a sign-back means you have technically won. The house is yours if you can live with the seller's response.

- **Be wise**. Investigate the reasons behind the listing. Some sellers are more motivated than others, such as in a divorce or job relocation, which means you can be even tougher in terms of price and conditions. Powers of sale are always the best kind.

A few tips on when to buy and when to borrow:

- Avoid the prime-time periods for residential real estate, which are February through May and September through November for houses, and March to July for cottages and recreational properties. This is clearly when you will face the greatest amount of competition; however, it's also when the greatest number of listings typically hit the market.

- Avoid getting a mortgage commitment during RRSP season, from New Year's through to the first of March. Every year billions of dollars in GICs mature around that period of time and banks, eager to retain that cash and compete with savings bonds, tend to nudge rates higher.

- Shop for real estate during the slow times, like statutory holidays and long weekends. If you are the only buyer showing up on the doorstep of a motivated buyer on holiday Monday, you may well be embraced.

- Be mindful of the school year calendar, which dominates the lives of so many people who need to move between the end of June and Labour Day. This can be helpful to remember when bidding for the house of people with kids. Make the closing date as convenient as possible and it can't hurt the deal.

The moment of truth

It's when you sign multiple copies of the offer to purchase, and it disappears into your agent's briefcase to be presented a few minutes or hours later. The offer is everything: The framework of a deal, a mechanism to draw the seller out and discover what he really wants as part of a dance, or a bold and decisive strike to get the asset you covet.

Face it: There is a certain element of confrontation involved here. The seller wants maximum dollars and minimum red tape. The buyer wants to pay as little as possible and have maximum protection. You know going into a deal that most of the time there will be a certain amount of back-and-forth. In a normal market where multiple offers are not expected, your document is intended to engage the seller and elicit a sign-back—at which point you realize that with your own simple signature, the deal has been done. It can be a very compelling moment.

I remember the emotion involved in signing the offer for my first home; my first investment property; my cottage; my first farm; my first commercial retail building. It is always the same rush of adrenaline as you go from being an interested shopper to a player willing to throw the dice on hundreds of thousands of dollars of cash or debt. Sometimes vendors are reasonable and react as you'd expect. Sometimes they are wildly unpredictable, which is why you should also have the wise counsel of an experienced agent when you consider a sign-back situation.

Offers are legally binding, by the way. Once you make a formal offer, it can be accepted instantly and you are required to go through with the real estate purchase on those terms. If you balk, and refuse to hand over the deposit or fail to ultimately close, then expect to be sued. The jilted vendor can go after you for damages and for the difference between your offer and what he or she will ultimately receive from someone else. But a sign-back offer can be allowed to expire with no consequences for either buyer or seller.

There are some things you have to consider before knowing how to put together a winning offer.

- **Is the seller motivated?** Then you can go in with a lowball offer, trying to scoop off the property at a bargain price from someone who's just happy to find a buyer. You can put in lots of conditions to protect yourself, such as a home inspection, and you can go after drapes, appliances, carpets, and so on. But if the market is hot, with competing bids, or if the vendor is just on a fishing expedition, then the offer has to have substance and appeal.

- **Are *you* motivated?** The strength of your offer should reflect the depth of your conviction about the property at hand. If you absolutely need to have it, then make the offer unconditional and at the best possible price point. If you are just dipping your toes in the market waters to test them, always give yourself an out, like making the offer conditional upon finding satisfactory financing, or upon the successful sale of an existing home.

- **What's the market like?** In a seller's market the offer has to command attention and be as simple and straightforward as possible. Give top buck to counter a bidding war. Include a fat deposit. Make the sign-back period short. Offer a signing bonus. In a buyer's market, take your time. Let your agent inform the vendor that something nice is coming, then wait three days to actually deliver the document. You'll be amazed at how much you win.

An offer can bounce back and forth between buyer and seller an unlimited number of times. On each occasion, changes are pencilled in and initialled, and a new deadline (called the irrevocable date) is established. The offer can be delivered by hand, on paper, or sent via fax or e-mail and, ultimately, you either cut a deal, or take a walk.

It's not uncommon for an offer to be allowed to expire, and then for the buyer to go after the property with a new offer a few days or weeks later. Your agent is the guy in control of this process—the one who presents the offer on your behalf, argues its merits, brings you any sign-backs, discusses the seller's position and mental state, and advises you on how to respond. At the end of the process, if a deal's been reached, your agent will deliver copies to your lawyer and your mortgage lender.

Having said that, there can be a role for direct negotiation between buyer and seller if things break down. I have done that on occasion in the attempted purchase of commercial real estate, where the issues are complex and the dollar amounts large. Sometimes there is just no substitute for a face-to-face encounter which will tell you quickly if there is a deal to be made or not.

Here are some common tips on putting together a winning offer:

- **Try putting in conditions you later remove**. In a normal market, where bidding wars are not forcing your hand, include conditions that you really can live without. It might be a condition to find good financing, obtain a home inspection, or get an updated survey. These conditions can easily be dropped on a sign-back, showing you are a serious and motivated purchaser, in exchange for getting a lower price.

- **Ask for everything**. Drapes, carpets, light fixtures, furniture—it's all fair game to include in an offer. Even where the seller's agent has excluded items, like a favourite chandelier, from the listing, you are perfectly free to claim them as part of what you are paying for the property.

Of course, it is assumed that some things go with the house, like broadloom, storm windows and screens, garage door openers, or anything else that is screwed down, nailed in, glued together, or installed. These things are called fixtures, as opposed to chattels, which is stuff that can be moved.

So, specify what chattels you want, including all appliances, the freezer or satellite dish, swimming pool cleaner, that power washer you spotted in the garage, or all the firewood piled in the backyard. The more you put in simply means the more wiggle room you have later to take things out—all in the hope of getting what you really want, which is the house at the best price possible.

- **Offer the right price**. Human nature dictates that the seller's eye will travel first to the line of the offer that spells out the price being offered, and this will colour his or her opinion of everything else—conditions, closing date, deposit, or chattels. In a hot market, make this the highest number you possibly can, since you probably will get only one shot. Of course, remember your limit and never exceed it.

  In a normal market, or a slow one, the amount offered should leave room for manoeuvring. Go in with a less-than-asking-price amount and see what happens. Certainly by making the offer clean of conditions, and accompanying it with a big deposit cheque, you increase the odds of paying what you want.

- **Upfront cash counts**. When it comes to dogs and deposits, size does matter. For starters, your agent will want to see a deposit big enough to pay for the commission generated by the deal. But beyond that, a big deposit will impress the vendor and attest to your seriousness as a buyer. It is also there (in the buyer's mind) as a windfall gain in case you take a walk, the deal does not close, and the money is forfeited to him. As well, the more cash you are able to throw at a deal, the less mortgage financing will be required, and the more equity you have in the real estate.

- **Mind the closing date**. Remember that your lawyer will need at least a month to properly search title on the property and perform the other due diligence tasks, like writing to the municipality and utilities to discover unpaid taxes, liens, or other little surprises. Your mortgage lender will also need a few weeks to approve the property and advance the funds.

  More importantly, you and the seller need to coordinate things to ensure an orderly transition. If you are a first-time buyer, then you should have more flexibility than someone selling an existing home and trying to juggle two closing dates. You can always use the closing date as one of the tools of your offer in getting a better price or other concessions. Don't be rigid, since bridge financing is relatively cheap if you're selling another home and the dates don't end up matching.

  Finally, never make the closing date at the end of the month, when registry offices are the busiest, when you might get dinged with more mortgage interest than you want, and when you certainly will have a heck of a time finding a mover.

- **Protect yourself**. Make sure to include in the offer an opportunity for you to visit the property two or three times prior to closing, upon reasonable notice. That will allow you time to measure for drapes or carpets, or to bring contractors through to discuss renovations. Never assume that a seller will allow you to set foot in the place one minute before all the money changes hands for fear you'll find something wrong. And, speaking of that, make sure to get a warranty—a clause that the seller guarantees that all the fixtures and chattels you agree to are in good working order on the day of closing. That way, if anything breaks before the deal closes, it's not you footing the repair bill.

Personal choices

For years now, my views on residential real estate and my predictions about where it is going as an investment asset class have been considered to be controversial. Naturally, my cautions about the challenges some kinds of real estate face have been misinterpreted. Some people just say I am negative towards it, which is completely untrue.

In fact, like you, I love real estate. Owning it can be exciting, rewarding, and profitable. In my married life I have owned eighteen pieces of real estate, from city houses to farms and commercial properties, and I am constantly on the hunt for more. Today 50% of my net worth is in real estate, and a little less than half of that is income-producing. And while my financial assets, like stocks and bonds, perform well in good markets and bad (thanks to my portfolio manager), the real estate side is a lot more fun. I can stand on the patio of the Belfountain Village Store on a Sunday afternoon, for example, and watch a fascinating stream of humanity flow across the property, in and out of the ice cream parlour, through the general store, and spilling onto the lawns. Not a day goes by that I regret having bought the place, despite the ongoing headaches of maintaining a 115-year-old landmark building that also keeps a dozen people working.

This is an example of real estate that makes sense. But residentially, there are also ways of making a property work for you by ensuring you buy what you can later sell for a tax-free profit. Let me recite this passage on my other personal real estate choices from *The Little Book of Financial Wisdom*, which I wrote following September 11, 2001:

> Let me tell you about my real estate, as I have made careful choices. I chose to get rid of a beautiful stone home in a prestigious area of midtown Toronto on a street lined with

The fun side of real estate: The Belfountain Village Store, where I watch the tide of humanity pass by.

houses fetching well over a million dollars. I downsized, and at the same time spent a small fortune building a home in the forest, on a river, an hour's drive away.

I spend long hours on Bay Street, running a company I founded which produces television shows and operates a broadcast centre. But commuting is not an option in a city which is forecast to have 35% more cars within the next ten years. Already the average commute in Toronto, one-way, is seventy minutes. Soon that will be ninety, which means suburban dwellers will routinely have to set aside three hours a day for travel. This is one reason suburban real estate sells at such a discount compared with urban properties, and why the gulf will continue to grow.

But while my vocation is in the city these days, my heart is not. Hence my place in the woods. But why tie up a million dollars in a city property that's used four days a week? And why not cash out of the kind of home that relatively few people can afford to buy, and may be an expensive white elephant in another decade?

So, I sold the kind of home now that may be tough to

sell later. I moved my capital into the two kinds of real estate that I believe have a strong future: a very private, all-year recreational property within an easy drive of the city core, and a no-care freehold townhouse with a backyard and underground parking, fifteen minutes off Bay Street. In the country I am comfortable and self-sufficient behind a gate I can open via the Internet, with a propane-powered backup electric generator, garden, wells, and a steep driveway that uses landing-pad technology to burn off winter snow. It has a separate guest-house apartment for visitors and is five minutes from the grocery store and seventeen from a hospital. I believe in a decade it would sell overnight. But I don't think I'll list it.

In the city, my condo townhouse is twenty feet wide and three storeys tall. It's four minutes from the subway and just off a major route leading downtown to the bank towers and uptown to the highways. Gardeners for the complex take care of the grass and flowers. In the winter the snow is removed and underneath is heated indoor parking. Garbage disappears from the back door twice a week, and yet I have my own fenced and landscaped backyard, which the dog loves and protects. The condo fees are cheap, the taxes a third of what I was paying at my old stone home, and I bought it for less than half what I sold the detached home for, just a few streets away. I believe in a decade this too would sell overnight. It has a huge universe of potential buyers who can afford it, and who want the convenience and the location.

There is smart real estate, there is excessive real estate, and there is real estate that has no future. There's a reason why tiny, sixty-year-old, 800-square-foot bungalows along forested streets in midtown Toronto sell for $350,000 to $400,000 while brand new housing in the suburbs, three times the size, can be yours for less. The bungalows represent what people want: location, convenience, and quality of life. Walk to transit and the bank. Access to established schools. Big old trees. This housing sells in hours, despite the condition of the homes, because buyers know you can always renovate but never re-create.

Today, the right real estate strategy starts with a recognition of where true value lies when it comes to housing in the future. There are some kinds of homes that will actually decline in value as the universe of potential buyers shrinks. A prime example is a multi-bedroom monster house with a three-car garage, Scarlett O'Hara staircase, and pool in the backyard, in a distant suburb accessible from downtown only by spending gruelling hours on an eight-lane "expressway."

As the average family shrinks in size and the population ages; as more people determine clearly that they want to be urban dwellers or nature lovers; as cities find it increasingly impossible to modernize and add to their transit infrastructures, real estate tastes will keep on changing.

So while the housing market today is relatively robust, thanks to a decent economy and cheap mortgage rates, the time is ideal to cash out of housing that has a cloudy future. Meanwhile, the time is always right to be buying what others will want, and value, in the future. That could be an inner-city bungalow, a well-located, carefree townhome or semi, a property in an adult community on a golf course or lake, a condominium (two bedrooms instead of four), a self-sufficient and secure country home, or an age-proofed home with wide hallways, lots of light, few stairs, and a voice-activated home management software installation.

In terms of investment real estate, do not make the mistake of buying a single residential unit to rent out. Today, virtually any single home or condo unit will not fetch enough money to pay much more than the mortgage, so you are basically just turning over dollars. That cash is better put into a hard-working equity mutual fund. About the only income-producing real estate I would consider now and into the future would be a multiple-unit apartment building. It can generally be bought with a small down payment, and can give you positive cash flow from day one, plus the ability to remortgage it in the future, taking out tax-free cash.

Think ahead. Choose wisely. The wrong property could be your own personal wealth trap.

Rules to buy by

Most people buy residential real estate based purely on emotion, without ever really thinking rationally about why they are doing what they're doing. For example, I have a friend who lives in a suburban community a distant two hours by car from the downtown where he has to go to earn a living every day. When I asked him why he bought a home there, the answer was simple: That's where his mother-in-law lived, and his wife wanted to be close.

The trouble is, in that location the home is a tough sell and will appreciate in value slowly, if at all. Meanwhile, four hours a day on the road is enough to eat a normal car every three years and run up a mountain of gas and maintenance bills. That real estate decision may make his wife happy, but it's hardly logical. Is that too callous a statement? Well, when you are dealing with the single most expensive asset of your life, representing the bulk of most people's net worth, then emotion has to sit in the back seat.

In the city, near my townhouse, for which I paid about $400,000, the lots are small in a neighbourhood which has traditionally been working class. These days, owing to its excellent location, more and more professionals are moving in and blowing apart the existing bungalows to build tall, new, skinny, two-storey homes. The trouble with this is that it costs about $350,000 to buy an old bungalow on a twenty-foot lot, and putting up a new home is expensive, since the lot is small and building is difficult. By the time the job is done, there is easily $650,000 invested. At that point, it is impossible to recoup the money spent since the house sits beside an older one worth about half, on a street that is still predominantly populated by seniors, considered by realtors to be full of starter homes.

So, that brings us to the rules of intelligent residential real estate buying.

- **Buy the worst house on the best street**. The most valuable thing about real estate is where it's located. Yes, the old adage of "location, location, and location" being the three cardinal rules of housing is as true today as ever. Real estate cannot be moved and it is worth what it's worth because of where it's at.

So, this is the first thing to take note of—not the condition of the structure that sits on that piece of dirt. I don't care what's wrong with the house, because it can always be fixed, rebuilt, repaired, restored, or replaced. However, a bad or questionable location can never be changed, unless you buy the entire neighbourhood and fix it up.

That's why you should buy the worst house on the best street, not the other way around. In every city and town in Canada, there are "demand" areas that are in demand for a reason—either they sit on a lake or river frontage; command views of skyline, ravine, or ocean; have peaceful, leafy streets; are close to the best schools or transportation routes; or are unique in terms of topography, history, or population. Whenever you can, get into one of these areas, and then sleep well knowing that you've already taken care of the resale value of your home.

When choosing a house, don't buy a corner lot because of reduced privacy and more traffic. Don't buy a house that sits near a major highway, or that has a bus stop close to your front door. Houses next to schools or retail stores will always sell at a discount to ones in the middle of a quiet residential block. When it comes to condominium apartment buildings, high floors always command more money than low ones. And forget buying anything that's near to a police, ambulance, or fire station; a hospital or factory; service station, or dry cleaners. Avoid neighbourhoods that are clearly in transition. Established, tree-filled areas will always be worth more than new, suburban streets with twigs planted along the boulevards.

Of course, what you buy will always have to reflect what you've got to spend. So, buy the worst house on the best street. Fix it up a little. Make some money while living where everybody wants to live.

- **Buy what you can afford**. That sounds like simplistic advice, but you would be amazed at how many people these days are not heeding it. With mortgage rates so low, and so many lenders offering variable, below-prime products, borrowing money has rarely been easier—or cheaper. With the prime rate in the 4% range as I write this, money for home loans is available all over the place in the 3% range, which means you can borrow $300,000 for less than $1,500 a month. Incredible! To qualify for that, your annual family income needs to be roughly $50,000, which happens to be a little below the average income in Canada.

  But what happens if interest rates return to more normal levels? Over the last decade, mortgages have fluctuated between today's 3% and 15% in the early 1990s. The average has been about 8%, which puts the monthly payments on a $300,000 mortgage at $2,300. To qualify for that mortgage, family income has to catapult to about $82,000. It's clearly worth remembering today that you are borrowing money at completely abnormal levels. A good rule of thumb is that a house should not cost more than two-and-a-half times your gross earnings; so a $50,000 wage-earner will most comfortably occupy a $150,000 home. The monthly mortgage payment, plus realty taxes, should not exceed a third of your income.

  Of course in some areas, like Vancouver and Toronto, where the average house prices in late 2002 were $370,000 and $260,000 respectively, many people will be forced to exceed those limits. Do so with caution.

- **Think resale.** That's right, even before you make the offer to purchase, think about how you are going to convince somebody else to buy this place from you. Canadians spend an average of about seven years in a home, and that period of time is shrinking quickly. Additionally, the population is aging, and nine million Baby Boomers—many of whom now live in suburban, multi-bedroom family homes—will be hitting their sixties by 2010. A lot of housing of that kind is going to come flooding onto the market, and many Boomers will be making the trip into urban condos, city bungalows, or semi-rural communities. In short, the market is going to see a lot of change in a relatively short period of time.

   Buying into a developed neighbourhood is a good idea because change will be unlikely, and most people like predictability when it comes to their personal home. Parking is a big issue, especially in urban areas where you may have trouble finding a buyer who wants to pay for a permit to park on the street. Be careful there are not easements or rights of way that affect the property, because these could cause legal headaches and impediments to finding a future buyer. Detached houses always sell faster than towns or semis. Buyers also like yards and gardens (at least they think they do, until it comes time to shovel snow, cut grass, and dig weeds).

   And be wary of really big houses with lots of bedrooms. That used to be a selling feature, but times are changing fast, as the makeup of the population changes. There are more small families today than big ones, and five-bedroom homes are actually harder to sell than ones with three. The fastest growing use of a room these days? A home office.

- **Pre-shop the Net.** One of the best applications for the Internet, as it turns out, is searching for great real estate. There are millions of listings across North America available to view every day. Some terrific Web sites are run by big real estate companies, like Royal LePage (www.royallepage.ca); some are giant aggregators of multiple listings (like www.mls.ca), and there are thousands of sites maintained by individual real estate agents, which deal in highly specialized types of property, like my friend Marcia Reid (www.marciareidcountry.com).

The Internet provides a powerful research tool for pre-shopping the market, locating schools, hospitals, and other services in a neighbourhood under consideration, or for simply seeing what you can afford to buy—and where. Many commercial sites link directly to mortgage lenders who provide instant pre-approvals, and also offer calculators showing what cash you need to buy a specific property, and what monthly mortgage payments will be.

Increasingly, sites offer pictures of properties for sale, along with a virtual tour providing a 360-degree view of the property or even streaming video, as well as the actual listing. Additionally, a lot of sites have popped up over the past couple of years that seek to put buyers and sellers together in a cyber deal that cuts out the middleman. For some people, I am sure that works just fine, but it's not for me. As much as you can learn online about a house, you should still employ a knowledgeable agent to help you buy or sell in the most powerful way possible.

Everybody needs an agent

It's not easy being a real estate agent. You have to find listings and you need to find buyers. You get paid when a deal closes, which can be months after you started to work on that project. Often you have to pay a broker for a desk, a phone, and part of the company marketing materials. Out of your own pocket you still have to finance everything from business cards to your Web site. There is no holiday pay and no pension.

No wonder the business attracts some of the purest entrepreneurs in Canada, people with confidence in their abilities and the courage to launch out on their own, with no safety net below. Those who work hard and achieve success can make fabulous amounts of money and have squadrons of personal staff. Those who can't bring buyer and seller together quickly fail.

Too many Canadians think of agents as salespeople rather than deal facilitators. And many people try to sell a property on their own, thinking they're saving tens of thousands of dollars in commission. Often, exactly the opposite is true. Do-it-yourselfers lose money because, without the benefit of an agent, they do not attract the widest interest or the greatest number of potential buyers, nor the best price.

For the buyer, using an agent to find a home and negotiate a deal is a no-brainer because the service is absolutely free—it's the seller who pays the commission. In fact, buying a house without an agent is a terrible idea, unless you relish the thought of spending a few weeks doing things you have no experience at and will probably screw up.

So, find an agent and then be loyal to him or her. Don't shop the market on your own while your agent is out trying to do it for you. For example, don't go to open houses without announcing that you have an agent or you might jeopardize the commission that will pay for the service you receive.

A good agent will question you about what kind of property you're looking for, in what price range, and in what type of neighbourhood. Then expect him or her to search the market using everything from the MLS system to a street-by-street canvass of property owners who might want to sell. Your agent will talk to other agents about new or potential listings and bring you the latest on what's available—making you instantly aware of what's hitting the market.

The agent will go to industry-only open houses that are held when a listing first comes out and report back to you on that prescreening process. You will also be given "comparables" in the neighbourhood being shopped—the prices at which similar homes sold over the preceding few weeks or months. That will usually come with a history of area sales, letting you understand the range of asking prices and the typical sale-to-listing ratio.

The agent will also know how long a property has been on the market, the circumstances of the seller, and the potential motivation involved—all valuable information in determining your buying strategy and the nature of the offer you'll be making. And, of course, the agent is usually the best possible source of information you can have on the area itself: schools, retailing, transportation, population mix, and future development potential.

Once you have narrowed in on a property, the agent will visit it with you, assess the condition of the place, and compare it with other candidates. The agent will be the one actually putting the offer together in a proper, legally binding way. He or she will then present it, explain it, and fight for it with the vendor's agent, bringing it back to you with a signature and any changes; advise you on what the other side wants; and suggest how to respond. The agent will also help you find a competitive mortgage, if you ask; find a home inspector and be there during the inspection process; or arrange for a mover or a contractor.

And, remember, you pay for *none* of this—one of the best consumer deals possible! Finally, when it's time to sell the place, who better to list it than the person who helped you buy it, and who understands all the intimate details of why it's a good place to live?

So, the agent is central to the entire real estate experience, and in every transaction I have ever done, I've been impressed with the professionalism and enthusiasm demonstrated. For example, there was the time I was moving from another part of the country to Toronto during a housing boom. The agent I hired met me at the airport with a wad of listings, an analysis of various neighbourhoods, a complete schedule of viewings, intelligence on houses about to come up for sale, comparables, maps, and recommendations. Seven hours later we drew up an offer, which was accepted as my plane taxied down the runway that night at Pearson International Airport.

Can you imagine accomplishing that on the Internet? Forget it. There is only one way to buy real estate, and that is with an agent holding your hand.

But how do you find a great agent? It's as easy as finding a good financial adviser, which means shopping around, asking for recommendations, and talking to a lot of people. Some of the basic rules:

- **Get an area expert**. Real estate is geography-specific, and in rural areas or inner city neighbourhoods you need someone who knows what streets or districts are in demand, or what potential neighbourhoods to avoid. Drive around, look at the "For Sale" signs, and see which agents seem to have most of the action. Call them. Or talk to people you might know in the area who have recently bought or sold. Do they recommend their agents? Go to open houses and chat with the agents conducting them. Contact the leading brokers in the area, and ask for an agent or two to be recommended for you to interview.

- **Go online.** The Internet will help you pre-shop an area and also give you an indication of who the proactive agents are—the ones with the most listings, the most effective Web sites, and the greatest sales success. Looking to move to Halifax? Use a search engine to find area listings, then e-mail a few agents, giving them details of what you are looking for, and see what the response is. It's easy to find those who know how to do business. They're the winners. Hire one.

Especially when you are moving into an unfamiliar area or city, the agent is your eyes and ears, representing your best interests and negotiating on your behalf. Be careful in the choice, then be loyal in the process.

Everybody needs a lawyer

Unless you live in B.C. or Quebec, you can't buy a house without a lawyer, and even in those two provinces you require a notary. But no matter where in the country you are, you are always better off with a lawyer, and obviously with one that specializes in real estate. An experienced guy can save you a lot of money by making sure the mortgage is properly handled, the title to the property is clear, and there are no lurking surprises like tax arrears or liens.

Your lawyer will talk to the lawyer for the buyer or seller that you're dealing with and, like your agent, his or her sole job is to look out for your interests. Expect a fair amount of paperwork when closing time rolls around, and (unlike with the agent) you will have to pay your legal fees on the same day you get (or sell) your home.

I like to use a lawyer at all stages of a transaction. Before submitting an offer, it's a good idea to have it sent to your lawyer for review. He or she may be able to suggest some clauses that will add to your protection, and if the deal is to buy a condo, then you definitely need a lawyer because of the added complexity.

It's also a good idea to have a lawyer in place before you even start shopping for a property. That's because deals can close quickly, in as little as thirty days, and you don't want to waste a week or so of that time trying to find someone to help you. In order to properly search title on a house and be in touch with all the necessary agencies, it takes at least a month. Get ready, then go shopping.

How do you find a lawyer?

Word of mouth recommendations are always useful, so ask

around among people you know. As well, every good real estate agent will know the names of competent real estate lawyers in the area, and that's an excellent source of knowledge. In addition, you can contact the provincial law society, which will provide you with a list of names of lawyers who specialize in real estate in your area. Of course, there's always the Internet, which will also give you names of lawyers and law firms that can help.

You might be tempted to just let the other person's lawyer (the buyer or seller you are dealing with) handle the transaction, but don't. That is a blazing conflict of interest that must be avoided at all costs. You have a very important personal agenda as a buyer or seller, and your interests are not the same as the person you are doing business with. Get independent counsel, and the best you can possibly find.

What's the lawyer's role?

There are several essential things that, as a buyer, you need to have done for you. For one, you need clear and clean title to the land that you are buying. Without that, forget even trying to arrange a mortgage. Any claims against the property have to be discovered and dealt with. Any issues that affect the property, no matter how old, could prevent you from getting title.

For example, that village store I bought recently looked like a simple deal. But my lawyer (a real estate perfectionist) found a discrepancy in the legal description of the lot the store sits on, going back to 1842. It seems that for the last 160 years nobody had bothered to clean up this problem and, had he not caught it, it might have prevented me from getting financing on the place in future. The offer insisted on getting clear title, which meant a new survey at the owner's expense.

Your lawyer will search the history of the property at the local land registry office (or online, now, in several jurisdictions), which will show you what previous owners paid for the place, when they put financing upon it, and how much. In addition, your lawyer will write to all the utilities to see if there are any unpaid bills. If so, they will be deducted from the proceeds of the sale going to the vendor. The same process takes place with regard to unpaid taxes. Your lawyer will seek to get a clean bill of health for the property, making sure it conforms to zoning requirements or, in the case of a country home, that the well and septic are legal and operational.

Is the house you're buying actually within the lot lines of the property it sits on? Is the property itself where it's supposed to be? Those may sound like dumb questions, but they are important ones. For example, one time I almost bought a house on a large lot with a nice swimming pool and a ravine behind it, until my lawyer nixed the deal. He discovered that a previous owner had cleared away brush and arbitrarily extended the rear fence line more than thirty feet into the municipally-owned wood lot. Worse, when another owner came to install the pool, he assumed the lot line was the fence line, and had the pool built straddling what was the actual lot line. Big problem. Big relief for me that my lawyer picked it up by insisting on an up-to-date survey which was at odds with the property description on the listing. In fact, that is something you should always have included in your offer: a good, modern survey, provided at the vendor's expense.

Additional lawyer work includes registering you, or you and your spouse, as the owners of the property, i.e., put you on title. This is important because, in case your marriage fails (a 50% likelihood these days), family law acts stipulate that real estate assets be divided equally between partners. With both of you as owners, your lawyer will register joint tenancy—if one of you dies, the other gets title to the property automatically, and free of any tax.

Then, of course, there is closing day, when the lawyer will thumb a file folder several inches thick on the table and ask you to sign a small blizzard of forms. There are closing costs to consider—legals, land transfer tax, disbursements, and so on—which typically amount to about 2% of the purchase price of the home. Make sure you budget for those in advance. Your lawyer will then meet with the vendor's lawyer at the registry office, most typically where the deal is recorded and keys exchanged. Some weeks later a document package arrives with a breakdown of all the financial aspects of the deal. Keep that safe for future reference.

The cost

It varies, but for a typical, non-complicated residential real estate transaction, expect a bill for between $500 and $1,000. Always ask upfront for an estimate of the charges, and also expect that this will be in the form of a flat fee. In other words, the bill won't go up every time you have a question. Expect to pay for a lot of irritating little charges as well, like long distance, couriers, and photocopy fees.

If the deal is more complicated, this can change dramatically, especially for a commercial property transaction. One that I bought recently cost me almost $10,000 in legal fees. I hated paying it, but it amounted to insurance against much larger, and more costly, future problems.

Everybody needs
a home inspector

Most people spend less time viewing a home before they make an offer than they spend shopping for a pair of jeans. And especially in a frenzied housing market like the one that developed after September 11, the actual amount of time spent inside can be measured in mere minutes. Sometimes there is no viewing at all!

So, how can you possibly know if there are termites in the basement, how many years of life are left in the roof, or if the furnace is a few gasps away from certain death? The answer is, you cannot. And yet you are about to commit hundreds of thousands of dollars in cash and debt to buy this property from perfect strangers.

That is precisely why everyone needs a home inspector—particularly now, when houses are getting so much more complicated, with digital appliances, high-efficiency furnaces, and enough plumbing for a small hotel. To properly inspect a home takes expertise and time—both which most of us don't have. So every offer to purchase should, in normal times, contain a clause making it conditional upon a satisfactory home inspection, paid for by the purchaser. In abnormal markets, when multiple offers are the rage, this condition may well have to be waived, in which case you take an inspector along with you when the first viewing takes place.

If you insist on an inspection and the seller refuses to allow one then it's probably time to start looking for another home. For example, I know one couple who, when confronted with a leaky and crumbling basement wall on their seventy-year-old home, opted to have three thick layers of rubberized waterproof paint applied to it instead of going with the $7,000 job to replace it. Once the paint was dry, they listed the home. It sold in two days. No inspection.

Some points to remember:

- **Be prepared**. Like a lawyer, it's advisable to have a home inspector lined up and ready to go before you even start looking at homes. That's because once an offer is accepted you will have, in most cases, less than a week to get the job done and remove the condition. The inspection itself will take a good chunk of one day, and then there is a report to be written. Finally, you need time to decide if you can accept the house in the state it's in.

- **Renegotiate**. If the inspection report is negative, suggesting that major repairs are required immediately or in the near future, then you should go back and reopen the deal. After all, it was conditional upon you receiving a report that satisfied you. This means you can try to force the owner to make the repairs called for, or the purchase price can be reduced by the amount necessary to get the work done.

  For example, a country home I'm familiar with, in a fantastic and unique setting, had a garage converted into a family room. The buyers hired a home inspector who was able to determine that the garage foundation was starting to heave. So the purchase price was cut by the $10,000 needed to fix the structure. Not only did the purchasers spare themselves the heartache of significant work right after closing, costing an additional $10,000, but they were able to get the major excavation out of the way before moving in.

- **Get references**. There is no licensing agency for home inspectors, which means there are some bozos out there purporting to know what they're doing. Unfortunately, I once hired one to do an inspection on a cottage I was buying. For $300 I received a glowing thumbs-up report on a structure that was held together with raccoon dung.

  So, do what I did not: Ask for references and follow up

on them, asking former clients if the report they received was accurate and useful. Find out how long the company has been in business, if it has insurance, and ask to see a sample report. It's always an excellent idea to ask your real estate agent or real estate lawyer to offer names of people they have worked with in the past. And, yes, years in business does matter in an unregulated industry.

More specific questions to ask: Are you a member of a recognized industry association? Are you affiliated with a contractor or renovator? How many homes have you inspected? Do you have experience with this particular type of home? How quickly can you get me a full written report? Can I come on the inspection? (The answer to that one has to be yes.) Are you familiar with raccoon droppings?

The cost of a home inspection will vary, depending on the size and complexity of the home, but budget for $200 to $500. If you are considering a rural property, add in some more for travel time, and also a check of the septic, well, cistern, and pump. The best expertise in a situation like that is local expertise.

- **Be there**. On the day of inspection, make sure you wander around with your guy. In addition to seeing the condition of the place, you will actually learn how your new home works. Once you move in, it can be incredibly useful to know where the circuit breakers are and how to use them, how to turn off the water to a sink, toilet, outside tap, or the entire house, how to know when the furnace filter needs replacing, or how to access an attic or crawl space.

The home inspection should cover everything from the foundation to the roof shingles, including electrical, heating, and plumbing systems; sewer and water connections for city homes; insulation; the basement (I once bought a home with a nice, carpeted basement floor, not realizing it was laid on a false floor a few inches above a constant pool of water—yeah, no inspector…); kitchen and bathroom fixtures; chimney; drainage patterns; brickwork; and driveway.

The inspector will tell you what repairs are needed and what they will cost, but he should not offer to do the work himself. The verbal report will be followed up with a written one. As mentioned above, you then decide if you want to accept the house with its faults, cut a new deal, or take a walk.

Be aware that in a slow housing market when offers are few and far between, you should give the vendors an opportunity of making the necessary repairs, otherwise their lawyer could come after you, accusing you of using the inspection clause to renege on the deal. Yes, that's what lawyers are for—to fight for the best interest of their clients.

Will that be new or resale?

This is a big decision, and you should make it rationally, not emotionally. Too many first-time buyers opt automatically for a newly built home, largely because they have no experience with home ownership, cannot fathom changing the wallpaper or moving walls, and they like shiny new appliances.

Unfortunately, when you buy a new home you are always going to pay the retail price, since it is worth the cost of the lot, plus construction materials and a little profit for the builder on the day of closing. It will take some time—perhaps five years or longer—for the market to advance, pushing the value of that place above what was paid for it.

With a resale home, things can be entirely different in a normal market. You will usually get a better deal—more house, dollar-for-dollar, in a better location. A resale home also comes with a track record, because it will have had several, maybe dozens, of former owners, and a long history of valuation. It is usually easier to estimate what its future worth will be. Resales also have a strong advantage because they sit in a proven location—an established neighbourhood that has infrastructure, mature plantings, a sense of community, and (most importantly) confirmed real estate valuation. Remember the cardinal rule: There is nothing more important about a house than where it is.

New homes, of course, offer the buyer worry-free living, since they not only have new heating, electrical, and plumbing systems, but they also come with a warranty. In Ontario, for example, the New Home Warranty Program gives buyers a blanket guarantee that anything that goes wrong will be fixed, for a specific period of time. New homes also have straight walls, burn less energy, offer big garages and backyards, and creature comforts like Jacuzzis. But the streetscape is probably devoid of big trees and the downtown is a distant commute away—unless the development is an urban infill, in which case, big bucks are normally involved.

In fact, when it comes to new housing, prices are high because of the escalating value of land and materials. So there is also less room to negotiate on price, since the builder is not in the business of losing money. You may also have some problems with the closing date if you buy a house from plans. In a busy market, the trades can get backed up quickly, and labour delays can wreak havoc, meaning potentially long delays in actually moving in. Additionally, contracts for new homes are long and complicated. There may be some significant restrictions on what you can do with your home when completed (don't paint the trim pink or even think about parking your boat in the driveway), and extra charges can materialize during construction. Finally, you could go six months or a year without sod in the front (as one friend did) when the market's busy and supplies run low.

When you buy a resale, these are the advantages:

- **Location**. The neighbourhood is already established. You can research your next-door neighbours or the traffic patterns. If anything bothers you, look elsewhere.

- **Extras**. With a resale, you can easily write in the broadloom, drapes, appliances, gardening tools, pool equipment, light fixtures, or whatever else you fancy. With a new home, you will be absolutely amazed at how much money is required to outfit it with life's little necessities, like garden hoses or curtains.

- **Closing date**. It is carved in stone, and you know precisely when to pack, order the movers, send out address change cards, and book some time off work, not to mention having the cash and mortgage ready to do the deal.

- **Improvements**. Buy a resale and get a paved driveway, thousands of dollars in landscaping, an established garden and patio, and a swimming pool or garden shed—all expensive add-ons with most new homes.

But, of course, it's still an older home, and the odds of having to replace the furnace or the air conditioner or the roof will be vastly higher than with a new home. So, many people—as I said, especially inexperienced homeowners—do opt for the freshly built house.

Rules for new home buyers

Okay, if you *really* want a new home, here are some key points to remember. First, this will involves a lot more work than getting a resale, so be prepared for what might be a long process that could involve many delays as the builder gets municipal approvals, deals with the trades, and prays for an uninterrupted supply of materials. And, as with a resale home, you need to have an agent and a lawyer lined up to assist.

- **Research**. It's a must, especially in large urban areas like Calgary or Toronto, where there are oodles of new home developments to choose from. You have to study the newspaper ads, visit sales pavilions and model homes, collect lots of sales materials, and do a lot of driving. Most new homes are in the distant burbs, and you have to physically visit each site to know whether that's an option for your commuting and your lifestyle. After all, if you are an intensely social animal, then living in a subdivision where people go from car to garage to family room, and where streets are deserted by day, is not going to work for you. Find out before you buy.

- **More research**. Visit the municipal offices and take a look at the official plan. You might not be happy to find out a big box retail development is planned within eyeshot of your new kitchen window. Home Depot and Canadian Tire are nice places, but not in your backyard. Also try to get an opinion on what the property taxes might be.

- **Investigate.** Once you have found a site that suits you, check out the builder. A good reputation and track record are vitally important, and the company should belong to a recognized professional group like the local home builders' association. Ask the builder's rep in the sales pavilion for references and the location of past projects. Take the time to knock on a few doors and inquire about the experiences of others who have dealt with this builder.

- **Choose the unit**...and do this carefully. There are many factors to consider, not the least of which is how many units are left in the development you are eyeing and how much you can afford to pay. A unit backing onto a ravine or wood lot will sell for more than one that backs onto another home. Cul-de-sacs come at a premium to through streets. Corner lots are less desirable. Lots with views—of fields, city skylines, water—will always be more precious. The decision you make looking at that diagram can have a big impact on the future salability and value of your new home once it becomes a resale in the next buyer's eyes.

- **Use an agent.** Yes, contrary to what most new home buyers think (because most are inexperienced), you always need an agent to represent your best interest while going through the buying process. This can potentially save you a lot of money and aggravation.

    An agent, unlike you, is a professional negotiator. He or she will go about the home purchase with dispassion and clarity. You will go about it in a state of emotional turmoil, making dumb decisions and being caught up with the colour of the bathroom tiles, when that actually doesn't matter at all. Remember that the person in the sales pavilion is paid by the builder and is probably commissioned. He or she is not working for you, so get someone who is.

Will there be some resistance from the builder or his rep? Quite possibly, but it won't last long since any potential buyer who shows up with an agent in tow is clearly serious. If the builder really wants to sell you a home, then he will pay your agent's commission.

Your agent will help you negotiate the best price, because all prices (new or resale) are negotiable. The agent will also work on securing the best closing date and ensure the contract is not completely one-sided in favour of the builder (as is usually the case). When it comes to financing, builders often have worked out deals with major lenders, like the banks, so it may be possible to get a preferred rate—your agent will ask for it, along with a deal to lessen closing costs. And your agent can negotiate for upgrades, like better bricks or thicker broadloom or a free fireplace and paved driveway.

It is always easier to have someone else asking those tough questions, while you just obsess about the tiles....

- **Consider a model.** Sometimes the best deals come when you buy an existing home that the builder has constructed as a model. In busy markets when buyers are swarming, models are unnecessary to generate sales, but when they are built, they can pose great value to a buyer. Often the builder has included a lot of upgrades and top-of-the-line home furnishings. Make an offer! Or you might wait until a development is mostly sold, then buy one of the last units from a builder anxious to wrap things up and move on—also at a discount. Conversely, early buyers (especially in large condo developments) can do extremely well, as builders court sales in the hope of getting some momentum going.

- **Use your lawyer.** Because the contract for a new home is complicated and almost always written by the builder's lawyer (on the best possible terms for him), you need your own counsel to make sure you have as much protection as possible. Get a lawyer familiar with new housing deals who knows about closing delays and what to do to shorten them. Show the offer to purchase and the contract to him or her before signing and make sure it gives you the right to inspect the construction site frequently, along with a final walk-through before closing. (By the way, never move into a house that is not 100% done, or you are moving into a giant potential problem.) The deal should also spell out what protection you have under applicable new home warranty programs.

Research, investigate, and negotiate, then enjoy the home of your dreams.

Is the condo life for you?

Condominiums have been in the news in recent years—sometimes for the wrong reason. In British Columbia, thousands of people lost millions of dollars in equity because they bought condos that turned out to be leaky. The situation became so serious that the government there launched an inquiry headed by former premier and MP Dave Barrett, which ultimately came up with a compensation package.

Barrett told me in an airport lounge in Vancouver one day that in all his years in politics, he had never encountered anything like the passion and rage of people who felt their homes had been violated and their finances shattered—by water. It turned out that construction techniques which work well in California and Arizona do not work on the soggy west coast of Canada, no matter how nice all those wooden exteriors look.

In Toronto, in the post–September 11 real estate boom, condos were again big news as they came to dominate new home sales in the built-up urban areas. According to the Greater Toronto Home Builders' Association, fully 80% of all sales in the 416 area code were condos, while the numbers were reversed in the 905 suburban area, where 80% were freehold. This is of great interest, since condos have traditionally accounted for just under 30% of the market, with one notable exception: before the great real estate collapse of 1989.

To be precise, a freehold home is one in which you own everything—from lot line to lot line, whether it's a detached home, semi or townhouse. You own the grass, driveway, bricks, shingles, windows, and walkway.

Not so with a condo, where all you own is the space between the walls of the unit, from the paint in, floor to ceiling. You also share in the ownership of everything else in the condo development with all the other residents, including the structure itself, the parking garage, elevators, landscaping, windows, and roof.

A condo can also come in lots of different varieties, not just as an apartment building. There are condo lofts, townhouses, commercial units, and rural communities with acres of common grounds. In Ottawa, I owned a condominium home which was part of a small collection of detached homes built in the 1930s by the man who developed the Cord automobile. For all intents and purposes, it was a regular house—except for the condo form of ownership, which gave me the advantage of no outside maintenance and daily winter snowplowing (which is a big issue in Ottawa!).

Typically, some of the common elements that everybody owns are set aside for the exclusive use of individual owners, such as balconies or backyards, lockers, and parking spaces. You buy, sell, and mortgage condos just like regular freehold homes, but you only insure the contents of your unit, while the condo corporation carries insurance on the physical structure itself. Condo owners pay a regular monthly fee for common expenses, such as outside maintenance, ongoing repairs, landscaping, utilities, and a reserve fund.

Like freehold homes, condos come in all price ranges and can be a great way for first-timers to get into the market, moving from renter to owner in a small apartment space. At the other end of the scale, you see older people selling off mansions which require lots of care and attention, and moving into luxury condos which offer a more liberating lifestyle. (The most expensive condo in Canada is proposed for Toronto—the one Donald Trump was backing—in a 60-storey tower. The price tag is $18 million.)

There can be distinct advantages to buying a condominium. For example, as mentioned, there is no outside maintenance to worry about—no grass to cut, snow to shovel, roof to patch, or driveway to seal. All of that work is contracted out and arranged for by the condo corporation's board of directors.

This means you can have an exceptionally carefree lifestyle in a condo, just shutting the door and travelling as you wish, knowing someone else is looking after the chores.

Also appealing is the stable nature of the ongoing costs of ownership. With a freehold home you just never know when the furnace may quit or the basement flood. With a condo, your predetermined monthly fee takes care of everything. Also speaking of money, often it costs far less to find a nice condo residence in a demand neighbourhood than a freehold home in the same location. You still get to enjoy the same streets, the same trees, shopping, proximity to work, or views as those who spent five or ten times more getting a house. Just ask the folks on the water in Vancouver.

Another big plus for people who like big swimming pools, exercise rooms, libraries, or art galleries is that condo developments often come with such amenities built right in. When everyone chips in through their condo fees, some impressive things can be built.

So, is the condo life absolutely ideal for everyone? Definitely not. Some people hate the loss of personal freedom that condominium living necessarily brings. Because you do not wholly own the unit you live in, you cannot control it or even change it without collective agreement. That means making no exterior improvements or even internal renovations in many cases. There can be lots of rules, and they can change at the whim of the people who control your corporation—condo owners themselves who may not share your vision, or who may decide that major renovations or improvements are required. The board can authorize that extra money be collected from all owners, or place a lien on your unit if you refuse.

There have been several instances in New York City of condo boards having jurisdiction over who can actually buy a unit in a prestigious building. Prospective buyers have to be sponsored by existing condo owners, then have their personal finances and habits examined to be eligible for admission! Less dramatic, but also important, are the possible restrictions that the condo board or bylaws of the condo corporation can place on ownership of a dog or a cat. The condo laws governing a townhouse I own in Toronto allow me to own "one normal pet." (My Siberian husky does not know this.)

Also consider that you may have less privacy with a condo than a freehold home, especially when it comes to apartments. Then there is the unit value itself to consider, since condos tend to fall faster in price when real estate markets decline, just as they can inflate dramatically in boom times. As mentioned above, condo construction can become excessive in hot markets, leading to an oversupply and years of price recovery.

If you are considering a condo purchase, make sure you employ a lawyer who's got some hands-on experience in this area, and who can guide you through the bylaws of the corporation before you make an offer. Find out what the financial situation of the condo corporation is and get a copy of its annual statement. Are there any major repairs pending or special levies?

In shopping for a condo, check out who manages it, and speak to a few owners about their level of satisfaction with how the exterior spaces are maintained. Have your agent determine how many units are vacant and what the past history of sales has been. Also determine how many are owner-occupied and how many are rented out. Determine if you will get an exclusive use parking spot, since this can be an important feature for resale. Can you lease out your spot to someone else if you don't need it? The bylaws will tell you.

And once you do buy, run for a seat on the condo board. It will likely mean one night's commitment every month or two, but it's well worth doing. The board determines how the entire development is maintained and makes decisions on repairs and renovations. Because those choices have a direct impact on your investment, you should be in the room.

Closing the deal

New or resale, freehold or condo, city or country, apartment building or estate, every deal has to be closed, and it's always going to happen in a few short minutes. Lawyers for buyer and seller meet, they exchange documentation and cheques, keys are handed over, and the deal is registered with the government.

The closing date is determined at the time you buy the property or the unit, and you must have all your ducks in a row for that time—all conditions on the offer must be met or removed (such as a successful home inspection or arranging of financing), your mortgage has to be approved and the funds advanced to your lawyer, your agent has to be paid, and you must be ready to move. Of course, never underestimate how much of a hassle that will be! One time Dorothy and I bought a home when I was a Member of Parliament and on the day of closing we arrived with our fully loaded moving van to find the vendors scrambling to move out. They had left packing everything up until the last minute and were disastrously behind schedule. We sat on the street waiting for a few hours, watching them throw things into the back of a borrowed truck, while our idle crew was costing several hundred dollars an hour.

In other words, it's always a good idea to have your agent stay in close touch with the seller's agent to ensure there is an orderly transition, so you avoid wanting to eviscerate the vendor (it's not a good career move when you're an MP).

Also important to remember is that closing a deal costs money—quite a lot, in fact. You should budget for added expenses equal to about 2% of the entire deal. So, on a $200,000 home, you need an extra $4,000 to get the transaction done. It is a nasty little surprise that has ruined closing day for a lot of buyers.

Where does all this money go? The biggest bite comes in the form of land transfer tax, which is a blatant piece of theft on the part of most provincial governments. Every time a piece of property changes hands, whether it is increasing in value or not, it is taxed. The tax rate also rises with the purchase price, and if the full amount is not paid on the day of closing, the deed cannot be registered.

You may also face a smaller tax bill for provincial sales tax on the value of any chattels that are included in the deal, such as appliances, although clever lawyers can usually stickhandle around this.

Speaking of your lawyer, he or she has to be paid. The legal fees cover reviewing the offer to purchase, searching title, corresponding with agencies and utilities, examining the survey, and dealing with the opposing lawyer. Certainly ask what the fees will be in advance of hiring the lawyer, to avoid sticker shock.

You will also be stuck for disbursements, which are payments the lawyer makes on your behalf. There may be a fee paid to the municipality to issue a tax certificate. The province needs to be paid for the title search and deed registration. The registry office also levies a fee for a certificate indicating their are no judgements involved, and you also have to get an occupancy permit for a new home. In addition, there will be courier costs, long-distance charges, and those infamous photocopying fees.

After the deal is done, you will get a statement of adjustments which shows exactly how much money changed hands and what it was for. The vendor will be credited with money paid in advance for realty taxes, or sewer and water charges, or the amount of fuel oil left in the tank in the basement. There could also be charges for a new survey or bridge financing. And when it comes to the mortgage, expect to pay for an appraisal done on the property and also mortgage insurance on high-ratio loans (more than 75% of the property's value).

So, make sure you understand how much extra money will be required to make the deal fly well before closing day, and have it on hand. It's a bad idea to just increase the mortgage amount in order to cover these charges, because you'll end up paying it back several times over in mortgage payments. But it's a good idea to check out a cash-back mortgage, now offered by most major lenders. Typically, you can get 3% or more of the mortgage amount paid to you, in cash, on closing, as an incentive for taking out the loan. On a $150,000 mortgage, that's a $4,500 gift that can come in very handy!

How to buy a cottage

Across the country, coast to coast, from PEI and Nova Scotia's South Shore to Muskoka, the Qu'Appelle Valley, Whistler, and Saltspring Island, recreational and cottage property is hot. Prices in recent years have shot higher along with demand, and this appears to be an area of real estate that is going to outperform for years to come.

In Ontario it's getting increasingly easier to drop a million bucks for a four-season recreational property on a lake four hours north of Toronto. In Whistler, you can spend three times that on a chalet in a town that somewhat defies description. As cottage and recreational property prices soar, there are more creative solutions coming to pass, like the time-share cottages on Ontario's Lake Kashagawigamog. For about $50,000 you buy one-tenth of a cottage which gives you the right to spend five weeks a year there. A full-time maintenance crew makes sure there are no chores to do while you're vacationing.

That appeals to some people but, to most, owning a cottage and probably passing it down to your children is a family dream. Today only about 7% of Canadians own a second home or a recreational property, but that number is steadily increasing. The major problem is that demand far outstrips supply, because, as a recent RE/MAX survey showed, more than 80% of cottage owners have absolutely no intention of selling their property—ever. It is this imbalance that has resulted in prices taking a giant leap forward. But there are also some other powerful reasons to consider buying a cottage as a sound, long-term investment:

- **Demographics**. Yes, the Canadian population is getting older and, traditionally, cottage ownership has been most popular among people aged fifty and older. After all, that's where the money is, and this is the group most able to afford a second home. Many of them do so with the intention of turning it into a permanent retirement home.

The big news here is the Baby Boom generation—nine million egomaniacal individuals who are all now moving into their fifties, many of whom have great childhood memories of poison ivy and spider bites at the cottage. This demographic tidal wave is starting to have an impact on the cottage real estate market, but the real effect is yet to be felt.

- **9/11.** Recent events, like the tragedy of September 11, 2001, have also had a profound influence on the cottage and recreational property market by changing many people's psychology. Some people have been reminded in a powerful way that everything can change in a single day, so why not go out now and get what you have always dreamed of, like a place on the lake or in the woods? As well, 9/11 did a lot to foster a sense of the importance of home and family, while reminding us of the inconvenience and danger associated with air travel. Both of those are positive for cottage life, and have coaxed people out of the city.

So, what kind of a cottage should you look for? Obviously you should seek out one that will both give you maximum enjoyment and also appreciate in value. The most important factor here is water. Cottages on a lake, river, or oceanfront command the greatest premium, followed by properties with a view of the water. Less valuable are ones remote from water or sitting in the middle of the woods.

When shopping, be careful that you research road access, as well as rights of ways and easements. Many lakes in Ontario, for example, have a sixty-six-foot road allowance running around the shoreline (a legacy of logging days), now owned by local municipalities. That means the land between your cottage and the water might not actually belong to you.

Here are some tips for the searching and buying process.

- **Always use a local agent**. You need someone who has an intimate knowledge of the area, of local prices, of individual properties, and the problems and attributes of that piece of cottage country. Drive around and look at who is selling what. Take out a subscription to the local weekly or daily newspaper and track listings, prices, and the realtors who have most of the action. Engage one agent to work for you exclusively, because properties can come on the market and be gone in a matter of days, or even hours.

- **Always get a home inspection**. Unlike in the city, cottage and recreational property owners are much more accommodating about accepting an offer conditional upon a satisfactory home inspection. That's because every property is unique; many have been built by former owners in stages over the years; and municipal building codes and bylaws have traditionally been a lot more lax than in urban areas.

- **Check out the mechanicals**. In the city you can assume the water will come in one pipe and the sewage go out another without any involvement from you, but not in the country. Most cottages have a lake or river as their water source, and you have to ensure the filtration or shocking system is up to the job. Also check out the pump and the pressure tank, and have a flow test done to make sure they're in good working order. Most properties have a septic system, which also needs to be checked out to ensure the weeping tiles are not cracked and environmental standards have been upheld. Make sure your lawyer gets a warranty from the owner that both systems are legal and functioning—and try to get that warranty to survive the closing date for a year.

- **Check out the quality of the water in the lake**, since that's what you'll be putting in your body. Some lakes have suffered from over-development, inadequate septic systems,

Cottages are in boom mode these days. Prices are rising fast, and if you can't afford a whole cottage, you can buy one-tenth of one for about $50,000, giving you five weeks of ownership a year. *Source: Chandler Point*

and the effluent from too many boats. Have a water sample taken and analyzed.

- **A survey is very important,** since many cottage properties end up in a border dispute. Don't buy a place that doesn't have a survey; or insist that the current owner provide you one, at his or her expense.

When you find—and buy—a cottage, chances are you'll be spending some serious money over the next few years fixing it up. Make sure you keep a detailed log of all those expenditures, along with receipts. Here's why: As a second residence (not your principal home), you will be charged with capital gains tax on the difference between what you originally paid for it and what you eventually sell it for. Over ten of fifteen years of ownership, that could amount to a whack of tax. However, you are allowed to deduct from the sale price all the money that you invested in the cottage by improving it. So, save those receipts!

Another tax advantage comes if you rent out your cottage for part of the season, which these days can bring you big bucks—up to $2,000 a week, or more, depending on the location and the cottage. While that income needs to be declared for taxation purposes, you are also allowed to deduct from your taxable income expenses incurred in owning the place, like mortgage interest, insurance, utility bills, and realty taxes. For example, if the property is used 150 days a year, and rented out for 50 of those, then 30% of all your cottage-related costs can be deducted from taxable income.

Finally, how do you finance a cottage purchase?

The easiest way is to use **savings**, perhaps cashing in your RRSP for the down payment. That may be raiding your retirement nest egg, but with the way the stock market has been going over the last few years, many people believe equity in a cottage beats equity mutual funds.

Or, you can get a **conventional mortgage**, on similar terms to those you have in the city. The big lenders have become a lot more accommodating than they used to be when it comes to recreational properties. In order to qualify, the cottage should be on a permanent road with year-round access; and your chances of getting a loan go up the more that the cottage is worth, and the more it has been winterized into a four-season home. However, expect to pay a little more in the way of interest than you do back in the city.

Or, you can use the **equity built up in your city property** to get the money to buy the cottage—with cash. All lenders will easily and quickly give you a home equity loan, and usually at the prime rate. You can borrow up to 75% of your city home's appraised value, assuming that it's paid for, and the money can be used to get that place by the lake. However, remember that the interest on a home equity loan is not tax-deductible in this instance.

The better-than-prime revolution

Over the past few years I have done a lot of work with the big mortgage lenders, largely because I am the founder of a television production company that turns out real estate programming. I routinely hook up with the head mortgage people at the Big Five banks, and get a lot of inside information on the business.

The news for consumers is nothing but good. The lenders are locked into a fierce battle for market share and are willing to give out some awesome deals in order to win your business. It's almost like mortgages are loss leaders to them—"relationship products," as they're called. Once you establish a mortgage relationship, then the odds are that the bank will end up with your RRSP, RESP, credit card, line of credit, and chequing account.

In addition, the innovations to the mortgage business are impressive, from one-minute approvals to 100% financing, and from mortgages that pay off your closing costs for you to ones that are automatically reduced every time you get a pay cheque. These days mortgages are flexible, portable, transferable, instantaneous, and, most importantly, cheap.

Interest rates in North America have been declining since the late 1990s, when governments were successful in killing off most inflationary pressure. The downward trend was accelerated unbelievably in the wake of September 11. In the hours following the terrorist attacks, the U.S. Federal Reserve, headed by veteran crisis-solver Alan Greenspan, flooded the financial marketplace with money to stave off a collapse, then immediately began dropping the cost of money to lower the odds of a recession.

As a result, interest rates fell to a forty-year low in the United States, and were still stuck there going into the autumn of 2002. Some analysts believe the cost of money will stay at that level well into 2003. In fact, there's reason to believe rates will remain at historically low levels for the next five, or even ten, years.

In Canada, the central bank followed suit, taking the prime rate down to 3.75% before bringing it back up slowly in mid-2002. Again, the forecast is for a very gentle set of increases, with the cost of money staying at some of the lowest levels in years.

For mortgage borrowers, it was a dream come true: The lowest interest rates in a generation, a new slew of bank products, and a mortgage war between the major lenders. Borrowing money just doesn't get any better than this!

The industry leader turned out to be CIBC Mortgages, which brought in something called the "Better than Prime" mortgage—a variable-rate product that offered a discount of 1.01% off the bank prime rate for most of the first year, then prime minus a quarter point for the remainder of the term. As the prime drifted down below 4%, it meant that a mortgage could be had for as little as 2.75%, compared with 14% a decade earlier. This put a house within the grasp of tens of thousands more people, and helped ignite a real estate frenzy that turned into an obsession after the events of September 11.

Soon all of the lenders were offering very competitive variations of the below-prime mortgage, and by mid-2002 more than 70% of all mortgage loans in the country were variable rate—the mirror opposite of what most borrowers had opted for just five years earlier.

But is it a wise move to go with a variable-rate mortgage that could jump higher if central banks decide it's time to cool off the economy with a round of rate increases? The answer to that is a resounding, "Yes." Here is why it makes sense always, but especially today, *not* to lock into the traditional five-year mortgage term. As I write this, mortgages with rates fixed for five years are available for just over 7%. Below-prime, variable-rate mortgages cost about 4%. Some people argue that it's good "insurance" to take the fixed term, because you have protection for five years from any increases in rates. But, figure it out.

If you borrowed $100,000 today at 7%, amortized over twenty-five years, after five years you would have paid over $10,000 more in interest than with a variable rate mortgage at 4%. That is very expensive insurance, indeed. Better to take that amount of money and put it toward the principal.

But what are the odds of interest rates rising steadily over the next five years? In my opinion (and that of just about every major economist in the country) the odds are extremely low. The consensus is for rates to stay flat in the States, and for the prime in Canada to rise to perhaps 5% by the end of 2002 and possible 6% by the end of 2003. The reason is that inflation is well contained within the Bank of Canada's target range of 1% to 3%, and technological advance is increasing productivity without increasing prices. Global free trade has heightened competition and opened new markets, which reduces costs. Meanwhile, governments have abandoned deficit financing and are reducing the national debt in both Canada and the U.S. That means no new government bonds are being issued, and the pressure on the money supply has eased off substantially. The bottom line: Low and stable interest rates for as far as the eye can see. Yes, the 1980s, with all that inflation, rising commodity prices, and 21% mortgage rates, aren't coming back. The smart money will stay with short-term or variable-rate mortgages and take advantage of it.

The best mortgage for today's environment is variable, and I encourage every new borrower or renewer to get a better-than-prime type product. Shop aggressively among the competing lenders, and once you have a loan, forget about whether interest rates rise or fall. There will be constant movement in the cost of money, but over the sweep of the next five or ten years, you will be saving yourself tens of thousands of dollars in interest.

How to get rid of it

Most people consider real estate to be a safe, stable, risk-free investment, as opposed to stocks or mutual funds. Ironically, however, people routinely buy houses with 5% down and 95% debt, making this one of the most leveraged investments imaginable. In fact, you can now get 100% financing from companies like Exceed Mortgage, as well as many mortgage brokers. In the United States, you can actually borrow 110% of the value of the real estate, which means somebody pays you money to buy a house.

But, debt is debt, and debt is bad when the interest on it is not tax-deductible. That is exactly the case with most residential mortgages, so the cardinal rule is this: Pay it off just as fast as you can. Getting a debt-free home should be your most important goal, and you can have no better financial plan than to get on a strategy to achieve that.

If you do not own a home right now, then buy one. With current mortgage rates the odds are you can own a house for the same money (or less) every month than renting an apartment. It's okay to purchase with a minimal down payment, so long as you do not increase your accommodation overhead. Don't make the common mistake of so many young people of buying a house and then spending the next ten years throwing every dollar they have into it. In a mildly deflationary world, with an aging population, real estate will not be the gold mine it was for the last generation. You also need money every month to buy financial assets and feed your RRSP.

If you have a home now and it is paid off, then today is a great time to take equity out. (More on that in a subsequent chapter on making your mortgage tax-deductible.)

If you own a home right now and it has a mortgage on it, then you should be aggressively reducing it, and increasing the equity in that property. This will multiply the number of financial options in your life. Here are some strategies for mortgage elimination, intended to save you a lot of money in interest payments:

- **Make pre-payments.** Most lenders will allow you, once a year, to make a lump-sum pre-payment of the original mortgage amount, typically 10% or 15% of the loan. That comes right off the mortgage principal, meaning it's paid off sooner.

- **Increase payments**. Another mortgage-busting method is to increase your monthly payment. Many lenders will allow you to double it, with the additional amount once again being deducted from the principal.

- **Shorten the amortization**. Mortgages are typically amortized (that's French for "killed off") over a period of twenty-five years. The lender gets most of his interest on the loan in the early years, which means for the first ten years, the bulk of your monthly payment is interest, and only in the final years of payments are you actually eating into the principal in a big way. By shortening the amortization, you will be facing higher monthly payments but getting substantial interest savings.

- **Top up payments**. Some lenders will allow you to throw in an extra amount against the principal whenever you have it, by topping up a monthly payment. In other words, your regular payment of $1,412 a month could be rounded up to $1,500.

- **Go weekly**. There is nothing requiring you to make monthly payments with most lenders. In fact, by accelerating your payments, you will save a ton of money and pay off the debt in a fraction of the time. This can be done by going from monthly to bimonthly, for example, but the technique really works the best when mortgage payments are made weekly.

The idea is simple: Take your regular monthly payment and divide it by four. Now make that payment every week and you will reduce the repayment period by about a quarter. It's almost like a bit of mortgage magic. Why does it work so well? Simply because there are more than four weeks in most months, so you end up making the equivalent of one extra monthly mortgage payment per year under this plan, which dramatically speeds up repayment.

Second, by making that extra payment early in the life of the mortgage, you are accelerating the reduction of the principal. Because it is lowered in size faster than with a monthly payment, the compounding effect of the interest is reduced. Remember, early mortgage payments are almost all interest, so if you can make payments more frequently, the small amount of principal being repaid is dramatically increased, dropping future interest charges on it.

But be careful when setting this up, because not all weekly-pay mortgages are the same. The ones that pay your loan off a lot faster are equal to one-quarter of a monthly payment, made each week. Some lenders offer weekly mortgages that are equivalent to the total annual mortgage payment (based on twelve monthly payments), divided by fifty-two. Do not be fooled by that calculation, since there is absolutely no benefit to you. The lender, however, gets the same amount of interest as with a monthly-pay mortgage, but more frequently.

For example, on a $200,000 mortgage at 5%, amortized over twenty-five years, the monthly payment would be $1,163. Divided by four, that would yield a weekly payment of $290. Fifty-two of those equals $15,119 a year in payments, versus twelve monthly payments of $1,163 which would total only $13,956.

To determine the exact savings in your case, plug into a good mortgage calculator. There are many of them available online, such as the Home Free Faster calculator, found at www.cibc.com/mortgages.

Remember that today's mortgage rates are a bargain, and lenders are offering some great deals as they continue to fight for market share. Shop around for the best rate; get a variable-rate, below-prime mortgage product, sticking with it even if rates rise; and use mortgage-killing techniques like lump sum payments and a weekly-payment schedule to reduce your debt quickly.

The best mortgage is a dead one.

More tips and strategies

So, you will ideally be walking into a variable-rate, below-prime mortgage with weekly payments. But there is something to be done even before you walk out the door to start house hunting, and that is to secure mortgage pre-approval.

These days, with an active real estate market, it is more important than ever to know exactly how much money you are qualified to borrow to allow for the fast action required to get the home you want. You can become pre-approved easily and quickly by visiting a bank branch, or doing it online. The advantages are significant:

- **You will know how much you can borrow,** so you'll know exactly how much house you can afford. Just add the cash you've got for a down payment to the mortgage amount and you have identified the top of your buying price range.

- **You lock in a rate.** The lender will give you a guarantee that on the day you become pre-approved, your mortgage interest rate is fixed, and will not rise over a set period of time, like three months. If rates jump during that period, yours will not. However, if rates decline, the bank will pass the lower rate on to you. How often in life do you get this kind of deal?

- **Pre-approval means you can eliminate the need for a clause on financing** when you go and make that offer to purchase. This strengthens your offer and puts you in a much more competitive position during a hot market. In fact, in any market, when you can eliminate the financing condition, you are better positioned to negotiate on other areas, such as price and closing.

- **Getting pre-approval demonstrates to your real estate agent that you're serious** about buying, and that may motivate him or her a little more to devote time to your needs.

It costs nothing to get pre-approved, nor is there anything stopping you from going through the process at multiple lenders, so you get the best deal. Even when you get pre-approval, there is no obligation on your part to actually go through with a mortgage. When you seek pre-approval, it's also a good time to run down the list of features that a lender is able to offer you. I've already written about options to pay off the loan as quickly as possible, such as weekly payments, pre-payments, lump sum payments, and shortening the amortization. There are other features you should consider, like portability (the ability to transfer the mortgage to another property, should you sell and move), cash-back (many lenders will give you 3% or more of the amount you borrow, in cash, on closing), split-level terms (the ability to carve the loan into separate terms, with differing rates), or protection in the case of illness or job loss.

How much money can you borrow to buy a home?

Banks will actually give you astonishing amounts of cash, because residential real estate is considered an exceptionally good asset to loan against. But there are some limits you should be aware of.

- A conventional mortgage is one that covers no more than 75% of the appraised value of the property. To get this, you obviously have to come up with enough cash to cover 25% of the price (plus closing costs).

- You can borrow up to 95% of the value of the home, and provide just 5% yourself. But any mortgage over that 75%

plateau is considered a "high ratio" loan, and you will be required to insure it, which costs extra. The two insurers operating in Canada are GE Capital and Canada Mortgage and Housing Corporation. The lender will arrange this insurance for you, and most people (unwisely, but out of necessity) add the insurance premium to the mortgage amount being borrowed.

- The amount of money you get is also dependent on your ability to repay it, so the bank will need verification of your income. The general rule is that you cannot have more than 30% of your gross family monthly earnings taken up by the mortgage payment plus realty taxes.

- Self-employed folks, entrepreneurs, owner-operators, and commissioned salespeople have long faced blatant discrimination from most of the country's lenders when it comes to getting a mortgage. While these are often the people who start companies, create jobs, give opportunities to others, pay big fees to the banks, and grow the economy, they have been considered second-class citizens and greater risks when they want to get a mortgage and buy a house. So, if you are one of these economic heroes, then be prepared to submit to the humiliation of having to provide years' worth of tax returns, to filling out a net worth statement, and undergoing vastly increased scrutiny. Ironically, any employee of an entrepreneur needs only a letter stating annual income to waltz out with a mortgage. Even more ironic, most owner-operators of small business today have more job security than the bank loan officers they deal with.

  One good development in this area is the SE85 Mortgage, which is offered by a progressive company called Home Loans Canada, designed to give the self-employed conventional loans, and treat them like real people at the same time.

A final note on mortgage strategies for people who were talked into taking long, fixed-rate terms and who have been watching in envy as rates dropped over the last couple of years. As mentioned, you are just about always better off with a short-term or variable-rate mortgage. But if you are locked in, here are some things you can do.

- **Blend and extend**. That means rolling your existing mortgage into a new one, with a longer term. The interest will be a prorated blend of the old rate on the remaining years of your term, plus a new, lower rate on the years you are adding. Some lenders will want to charge you a penalty for this, but you should probably be able to talk your way out of it.

- **Break the mortgage**. It is normally possible to get out of a long-term fixed rate to take advantage of lower rates, but it will cost you to do so. Expect to pay a penalty equal to the greater of three monthly payments, or the interest rate differential—the amount of interest between the existing mortgage rate and the current one on the amount of your principal over the amount of time remaining on your term. Once you figure that out, you realize there is no advantage to doing so, unless you believe mortgage rates, which are low now, will rocket higher in the future. But I don't think that's going to happen.

One other technique for getting out of an existing high-rate mortgage: Offer to borrow a lot more money at current rates. They usually can't refuse.

Make it tax-deductible

Yes, it is possible to have a tax-deductible mortgage in this country, and enjoy what the Americans have lavished in for years—the ability to deduct all that mortgage interest from your taxable income. Since most of your payment is interest, that is a windfall which will surely increase your wealth by slashing your tax bill.

As I spelled out in *The Little Book of Financial Wisdom*, the key lies in this fundamental principle: If you borrow money to create more money, then the interest is tax-deductible. That is the logic behind General Motors borrowing millions to build a new factory: The interest is a legitimate business expense and can be used to increase profitability by reducing taxes. The same goes for you. Borrow money to invest in the economy and receive growth on it, and the interest is a legitimate expense in your hands.

But there's a lot of controversy and confusion over this point and, in my opinion, it appears the blame for it lies squarely on the head of the Canada Customs and Revenue Agency (CCRA), formerly known as Revenue Canada. The CCRA has failed to amend wording in its annual tax guide that is totally misleading. Here it is, under the heading of Carrying Charges and Interest Expense, line 221: "You can claim the following carrying charges and interest you paid to earn income from investments: most interest you pay on money you borrow, but generally only as long as you use it to earn investment income, including interest and dividends. However, if the only earnings your investment can produce are capital gains, you cannot claim the interest you paid."

Sadly, that little exercise in jargon has scared a lot of people away from borrowing for investment purposes, believing if they buy stocks or mutual funds that do not pay interest or dividends, the interest is not deductible. But it is. Any financial adviser, tax lawyer, or accountant will set you straight.

Equally wrong is the warning contained in some of the tax preparation software packages on the market, which say: "If you borrowed money to invest in stocks or mutual funds that do not earn interest or dividend income, you cannot deduct the interest you paid on your loan."

That is an incorrect interpretation of CCRA's badly worded statement. Ignore it. Better still, throw out the software and let a professional do your taxes. Write this on a piece of paper and tape it to the fridge: "Interest on money borrowed to invest is tax-deductible." End of story. Now, on to your mortgage.

There are two strategies I like for creating a tax-deductible mortgage.

Asset Swap

If you have an existing mortgage on your house, you can make all or part of it tax-deductible through an asset swap. Now most people who have mortgages also have various forms of investments, like mutual funds. The idea is to take these assets and swap them for mortgage debt.

Do it this way:
1) Sell your investment assets. Cash them in, being mindful there will be a small tax bill to pay on any capital gains you realize.
2) Use this cash to pay off your residential mortgage (or a portion of it).
3) Arrange a new mortgage.
4) Use the new mortgage money to buy back the investment assets you originally sold.

Now you still own an equal amount of investment assets, and you still have a mortgage on your home. But because you borrowed against your home (in the form of a mortgage) in order to buy assets that create wealth, the interest on your mortgage is now tax-deductible. You have just given yourself a giant tax break.

Home equity loan

If you live in a house with no mortgage, it's even easier to build wealth and still get a fat tax reduction by using a home equity loan.

This is getting more common all the time, as the major lenders create products that allow you to tap into all those mortgage payments you made over the last few decades. You can generally borrow up to 90% of the appraised value of your home with an equity loan. The good news is that because the loan is well secured by the real estate, you can get it at a rock-bottom rate of interest, generally the prime rate. Even better news: So long as the money is used for investment purposes to create wealth you'll be taxed on later, the interest can be written off.

To make this simple and effective, most lenders will allow you to have interest-only payments, which means you never actually pay back the principal amount borrowed. But why would you want to, when the entire cost to you is deductible from your personal taxable income?

So, instead of just having a house with no mortgage, you end up with an investment portfolio that could be worth tens, or hundreds of thousands of dollars, plus the ability to substantially reduce your taxable income.

A home equity loan is not a mortgage, but rather a secured line of credit, backed by your real estate. The interest rate on the line will be variable, floating up and down with the prime. As I have argued elsewhere in this book, I believe interest rates will remain low and relatively stable, so no need to worry about escalating costs. In any case, so long as the money is used in the right way, all interest costs are tax write-offs.

As I write this, the prime rate is 4.5%, which means for

someone in the top tax bracket, half of the cost of the loan comes right off the income taxes you remit. That would be akin to borrowing money for investment purposes at half off the prime rate, which means this capital is actually costing you just 2.25%.

To deduct the mortgage interest from your taxable income, simply fill out Schedule 4 of your income tax return, indicating the total payment made during the year on your loan, then write the amount in on the appropriate line of the return. This is a deduction from taxable income. So, a $10,000 entry will reduce the final amount of tax you pay by $5,000 for someone in the top tax bracket in most provinces.

Going in reverse

For most Canadians, the biggest financial asset they'll ever get their hands on is their principal residence. Meanwhile, the vast majority of people have their mortgages paid off by the time they reach the age of sixty. That means millions of people are sitting on billions of dollars in home equity, many of them living poorly because they have lousy pensions and inadequate government benefits.

In the previous chapter I explained the benefits of tapping into that equity through a home equity loan or a secured line of credit, especially for investment purposes. But, this is not appropriate for everyone, especially risk-averse seniors who want both financial security and the ability to live in their own home.

So, a reverse mortgage, provided by the Canadian Home Income Plan (CHIP), may be a worthwhile option. The idea is simple: You are allowed to borrow money, tax-free, against the equity you have created in your home. You can use the cash to do whatever you want with, and there are no repayments so long as you stay in the home. If that sounds too good to be true, it almost is.

With a normal mortgage, a lender gives you money secured by your real estate, and then you spend the next twenty-five years paying it back, along with the interest compounding on the principal. If you take the full quarter century to repay, you'll pay back about three times the amount you actually borrowed. With a reverse mortgage, you receive money secured by your home, but there are no repayments. So what about the compounding interest? That is added to the outstanding loan amount, and it must be repaid when you sell the home. More on that in a moment.

Here are some of the significant features of a reverse mortgage:

- You have to be at least sixty-two years old to qualify.

- You can borrow between 10% and 40% of the value of your paid-up home, as opposed to up to 90% with a home equity loan or secured line of credit.

- The amount of money CHIP will give you is determined by your age, gender, marital status, and the value, location, and type of your home. The younger you are, the more you get. Women qualify for more than men. Freehold homes receive more than condos.

- There is a set-up fee to pay of about $1,700, as opposed to $300 to $500 in fees for a line of credit or home equity loan.

- Interest on the money you borrow compounds semi-annually, and is added to the outstanding balance, unless you decide to repay it once or twice a year. You also have the option of repaying the reverse mortgage at any time, but if repayment takes place in the first three years, expect a penalty.

- The rate of interest is set annually, as opposed to the constantly fluctuating variable rate on a home equity loan.

- The money you get is yours tax-free (since no capital gains tax is applicable on a principal residence), which means it is not counted into your income. As a result, this will not affect eligibility for government benefits, such as Old Age Security.

- If you use the reverse mortgage money, or part of it, to buy investments that will pay you income, then some or all of the interest that compounds on the loan will be tax-deductible in your hands—just as with a secured line of credit or home equity loan. That can offset your income tax payable and increase your cash flow.

- There are no restrictions on how you can use your reverse mortgage money.

- However, to get it, there can be no outstanding loans, mortgages, or other debts which are secured by your real estate. That also means property taxes, insurance, and condo fees have to be paid in full, and the property must be properly maintained.

- The title to your home remains in your hands, so you can sell or move whenever you want.

- The reverse mortgage lender has no right—*ever*—to force you to repay the loan in full, or to sell your home and move out.

So, how do you pay back this money? Typically, it will come out of your estate—upon the death of the last surviving spouse. Or, if you choose to sell your home, repayment will be made from the proceeds of the sale. In the case of an estate, there can even be some benefit in reducing probate fees, since the principal and accrued interest is deducted off the top from the total value of the estate.

But this is also the controversial part, because a reverse mortgage that has been in place for many years can build up a substantial amount of interest—which can have a serious draining effect on your estate. Should you be planning to pass along a lot of money to your kids, a reverse mortgage may not be for you. If you hate your kids, however, it's perfect.

How (and when) to sell

Chances are that every piece of real estate you ever buy you will also have to sell. Sometimes selling can be hell on wheels; sometimes it's amazingly positive. Like most people who have owned a lot of real estate, I have experienced both conditions.

For example, after the federal election of 1993 I found myself abruptly unemployed. Within a few weeks I had found work with a television network that wanted to me relocate to London, Ontario. The problem was I owned two houses, one in Ottawa and the other in my former riding, outside Toronto. The economy at that time was rough, mortgage rates were in the double digits, and we were just starting to come out of a horrible real estate market in which prices had eroded badly.

But I had to sell. I had no choice. So I moved to my new job, rented a house, and waited seven agonizing months until the other properties sold—both for less than I had paid. The buyers of those houses (one of them was the prime minister's spokesman), got a heck of a deal from a very motivated seller.

Four years later, the shoe was on the other foot. I had moved to Toronto for a better job, bought a home in a nice area for about $500,000, and then decided to sell and move up. The economy was in great shape, mortgage rates had tumbled into the 5% range, and investor confidence was running high. My agent listed the home and allowed showings to take place for a couple of days while I was out of town in Vancouver. According to neighbours I later spoke with, the street was actually completely blocked with the cars of prospective buyers. My agent described the scene as "wild," with entry to the house restricted to a few couples at a time.

In that seller's market, we ended up with seven offers, all of them for more than the asking price, and sold for a profit of almost $120,000—tax-free, of course. It was some of the easiest money I ever earned.

In other words, timing is everything. And, as I write this, a seller's market rages, as it has since early 2001, and especially since the world changed on September 11 of that year.

Going forward, I expect these conditions to remain largely intact as mortgage rates remain near generational lows, as the economy continues to grow, and as consumer confidence returns with the inevitably rising equity markets. It is a good time to sell, and a tough time to buy. Personally, I think it's a wonderful time for sellers to lock in real estate profits and for some people who live in the wrong kind of real estate to bail out.

Here are the fundamentals of being a successful seller:

- **Pick the right agent**. This is just as important to you, the seller, as it was to you, the buyer. Your agent should have intimate knowledge of the neighbourhood and, in the best of all worlds, he or she is the one who helped you buy the same property. The best agent will know by heart what most houses on the street sold for. He or she will be from a local office and maybe live in the same area.

  The agent must also have a marketing plan that should be shared with you from the outset. There should be at least one open house staged for interested agents, along with a listing on the MLS, Internet marketing, and newspaper advertising. The ideal and well-networked agent will likely already have a few people interested in the area—especially in a hot market, in a demand area.

  You can certainly interview several agents before engaging one, asking about experience, marketing style, familiarity with the area, and resources. The agent will tell you what he or she thinks the market value of the home is, but don't let that blind you. Some agents will give you a high number just to get the listing, and if it's the wrong number, the property will go stale and take much longer to sell.

- **Get the right commission**. All commissions are negotiable, regardless of what some real estate boards want you to think. It used to be that 6% was carved in stone, but these days you can find agents happy to go with half of that.

  And while you should ask for the best commission rate possible, it would be wrong to sign on with an agent based solely on that. A good agent will earn her or his commission by selling your house for a fair price in as short a time as possible to a qualified buyer. Your agent has a lot of work to do: setting the price, listing the home, marketing it, hosting other agents and potential buyers, working at all hours of the day and night and weekends, paying for the ads, preparing feature sheets, handling the negotiations, coordinating events between you, your lawyer, and your bank, and holding your hand.

  And then, the commission you pay is typically split between the agent and his or her office, and often between the buyer's agent and his or her broker. Would you work that hard for that little?

  By the way, with the rise of the Internet, there are more and more marketing companies trying to use the World Wide Web to replace agents by providing a forum in which buyers and sellers meet. You can certainly try one of these out before listing your home, but always realize your chances of getting the most money for your house rise with the greater number of people exposed to it. Today, hands down, that is through the efforts of an agent.

- **Set the right price**. I'll say it again: The biggest mistake you can make is pricing your house too high. It will get stale, be ignored, and require a markdown. You will take a lot longer to sell, and probably will end up with less.

  Instead, you are better to go to market with a house priced below its fair value, especially in a hot market. That is sure to attract attention and pump up the chances of getting multiple offers and competing bids all above the asking price. That's exactly the technique my agent used when I sold that Toronto house noted above.

A good agent will not just pick the house price out of the air, but rather base it on the recent selling price of a number of comparable properties in the area, combined with the relative advantages or disadvantages of your place. As I have also said before, regardless of how fantastic your house is and how much money you put into renovations, its worth is largely dictated by where it is.

- **Be proactive**. There are lots of things that you, the seller, can do to help your agent get rid of the place fast, for the most bucks. For example, make your home look its best by cleaning up the yard and moving around furniture to make the interior look as spacious as possible. You might actually put some furniture in storage to open up the inside, since the buyer doesn't care about your things—just the house.

  Pay for carpets to be cleaned and the walls painted, if necessary. Hire somebody to do the windows, and repair everything that's broken: doorknobs, screens, steps, etc. Paint the front door. Clean mirrors. Empty closets. The place cannot be too clean, especially for potential buyers who will stick their noses anywhere, including inside the shower and your oven.

  Make it easy for the purchaser to buy your house. Have an up-to-date survey ready. Be flexible on the closing date and have details at hand about your mortgage—can it be easily and quickly discharged, or is it assumable by a new owner? Have a year's worth of utility bills and tax bills handy to show what the costs of ownership are. Work with your agent on preparing a great feature sheet or four-page brochure, with colour pictures, attributes of the house, and details about the street, local schools and shopping, and the neighbourhood. Include seasonal shots—if it's winter outside, have some summer pictures. You can create this masterpiece easily on your home computer. A feature sheet or brochure is an important memory aid to buyers who might look at ten or twenty properties before making an offer.

Also a good idea: receipts for recent renovations, to show what value the buyer is getting, as well as the home inspection report you had done when you bought. Or maybe it would be a good investment to hire a home inspector when you list the house, so any potential buyer could have access to the report.

- **Pick the right offer.** In a seller's market the object is to get multiple offers, if possible, so it's important to pick the right one—which may not be the person offering the most money for your home. You have to take into consideration the size of the deposit (big is good), what conditions may be attached (the best offer will have none), the fixtures and chattels requested, the closing date—and the money offered. As the seller, you're always in a position to sign it back on your own terms, giving the purchaser a few hours to respond.

Real estate
with a future

Real estate, as mentioned, is a commodity. Its worth is determined by location and condition, but mostly by supply and demand, which is dictated by everything from interest rates to job creation, economic conditions, the weather and media headlines. The housing market is intensely local, constantly changing, and largely unpredictable.

But that does not mean there aren't trends that can guide astute buyers and sellers. There are, and they're powerful. The one that will come to affect real estate the most is demographics, which is the makeup of the population. According to 2001 Census data, the country is aging at the fastest rate in history. The median age of a Canadian is now closing in on forty years. The number of eighty-year-olds is bounding higher, and the fertility rate has plunged.

The nature of families is changing, as the marriage rate steadily drops and the divorce rate rises. The number of two-person families is exploding higher and the average family has gone from four people in 1961 to just 2.5 people today. Life expectancy has reached the highest point ever, with a girl being born today having an excellent chance of achieving 100 years. My own father died at eighty-five and my mother, at eighty-eight, is jetting around to Europe, Cuba, and across Canada.

What are the implications for residential real estate? With the Baby Boomers entering their fifties (all nine million of them), and the nature of families changing so dramatically, the taste for traditional, multi-bedroom, suburban real estate—which is still being built on huge tracts of land outside cities like Toronto and Calgary—will surely wane over the next decade and a half. That kind of housing has been, and is being built for nuclear families with two parents, two kids, and two incomes. But in the future a family is actually more likely to be a working, childless couple, a single mother, a young couple living with parents, two Boomers with a thirty-something child at home with no intention of leaving, or a gay couple with an adopted child.

This leads me to conclude that a lot of existing housing is going to get dumped on the market over the next ten years by Boomers in their fifties who don't need four bedrooms, but who do desperately need to raise retirement capital. After all, the average RRSP in this country contains just over $40,000, and about half of us have neither an RRSP nor a company pension. Meanwhile, most families continue to have the bulk of their net worth in residential real estate. So, figure it out. Big changes are coming. If you own that kind of real estate, then the time to get out could hardly be better today. If you are contemplating buying real estate, then you should make sure it's the kind that has a future, and will stay in demand. For example:

- **Urban bungalows, semis, and towns**. Why is it that a tiny 800-square-foot bungalow on a thirty-foot lot in Toronto's midtown Leaside district is selling these days for $350,000? For the same money you can drive thirty minutes away and buy a 2,500-square-foot, two-storey house on a huge lot. The reason is that these bungalows have what it takes: Location—a great neighbourhood, access to transportation and health care, and ease of maintenance. They appeal to people in retirement and to small, young families. They are ideal for a single person to live in, or someone who is disabled and in need of special care.

  This is the kind of housing that has a future, and will not only maintain its value, but grow it over the years to come. Here you don't need a car. You can walk to the Loblaws, the bank, or the library. Property taxes on the small lots are low. There are no stairs to worry about.

Bungalows are starting to make a big comeback in popularity, after being shunned and ridiculed over the last couple of decades. New bungalows are the hottest form of housing in developments being built and planned for those waves of retirees about to sweep across Canadian society—whether they are in the city or in rural communities.

- **Condominiums**. As noted elsewhere, condos are enjoying the biggest boom in almost twenty years, serving several distinct sets of buyers: first-time homeowners, move-down retirees, urban professionals, and investors buying one or twelve units to rent out.

  Condos come in many forms—townhouses, semis, detached homes, and rural enclaves—but most are high-rise, apartment-style complexes, all offering a carefree lifestyle devoid of maintenance responsibilities. They also give owners a heightened level of personal security, elaborate recreational facilities, the potential for worry-free travel, a sense of community, a warm, indoor parking spot, and a generally lower price than a freehold home in the same location. Are these not precisely the things more and more people will be looking for?

  Coming now is a housing form that has a great future: condo communities, geared to retirees who want convenience, service, and also independence. One such place outside Toronto offers residents five acres of gardens around their condos, along with a cafe, lounge, bank, medical centre, beauty salon, and market. Housekeeping and laundry services are available, and everybody's TV set features a channel to view images from the security cameras. It's like living in a village, a hotel, and a fortress at the same time. It changes and challenges our notion of condominium living, and it is the future.

Boomers, prepare to chauffeur your parents

Analysis

BY ANDRÉ PICARD
PUBLIC-HEALTH REPORTER

Parents looking forward to the days when they no longer have to strap their children into car seats and drive them endlessly to various events had better temper their enthusiasm.

Research suggests that baby boomers will act as unpaid chauffeurs for many years to come. But it will be seniors, not children, they will ferry.

"Hundreds of thousands of older people quit driving each year and must turn to alternative transportation," said Dan Foley, a biostatistician at the U.S. National Institute of Aging. "I don't think enough attention has been paid to the transition from driver to non-driver in the aging population."

His study, published in today's edition of the American Journal of Public Health, reveals that while people are living longer, they do not necessarily drive longer.

The gap between life expectancy and "driving expectancy" is about 10 years and growing. That means most seniors will be dependent on transportation other than their cars for more than a decade, on average.

The U.S. study reveals that about 600,000 people over age 70 give up driving each year (which translates to about 60,000 in Canada). About half of that number die or are incapacitated, but the balance are generally healthy, though they may be unwilling or unable to drive because of poor vision, memory impairment or limited mobility.

Given that public transportation in many areas is poor and often not suited to the needs of frail seniors, the burden likely will fall on family members, Mr. Foley said.

He said that the ability and willingness of older citizens to drive has important public-health implications because so many people are dependent on their vehicles. "Driving has an essential role in helping older men and women live independently."

Measures should be taken to ensure that people's health does not suffer when they give up driving and that older drivers don't take unnecessary risks because they feel there are no alternatives, he said.

In Canada, much of the debate about older drivers has centred on licencing, fuelled by accidents involving motorists whose competence to drive is called into question. But little discussion involves altering the rules of the road to accommodate the growing legions of older drivers and in financing alternative transportation, Mr. Foley said.

'Driving has an essential role in helping older men and women live independently.'

The research published in the American Journal of Public Health reveals that about 10 per cent of drivers are over 65, a number that is expected to more than double in the next decade as baby boomers reach the milestone.

Mr. Foley found that few people stop driving in their early-retirement years. Overall, 82 per cent of men and 55 per cent of women over the age of 70 drive. By age 85,

more than 55 per cent of men and 22 per cent of women drive.

Mr. Foley said the key number is the gap between life expectancy and driving expectancy.

On average, a 70-year-old man can expect to drive another 17 years. But according to the data, he is likely to drive for only another 11 years.

The driving gap is more pronounced with women: A 74-year-old woman can expect to live 21 more years but is likely to drive for more than 11 years.

According to the Canada Safety Council, the aging of the driving population should be considered as one of the country's top safety and public-health issues.

The council does not support restrictions on elderly drivers, but it urges them to take refresher courses that help adjust their driving to age-related changes.

Most provinces do not place restrictions on older drivers until they reach 80, at which time they must be tested. The number of road fatalities in Canada has dropped significantly over the past decade in all age groups except that of 65 and over.

Be prepared to drive your parents everywhere, especially if they happen to live in the wrong place for seniors—like the suburbs. *Source: The Globe and Mail*

- **Golf towns**. The Baby Boomers will be a real estate force for the next two decades, as they age but remain one of the healthiest and most active generations in history. Golf will be a huge industry as it gets millions more devotees. Many of them will want to live near a golf course.

This is consistent with the upbringing of a majority of Boomers as children of the suburbs, raised in a car culture, used to lots of space and personal freedom. Freehold homes on condominium land in golf towns, clustered on the perimeter of the city, will offer space, frontage, and recreation, without the drone of yard work or snow shovelling. These kinds of communities are starting to be built now, in the Lower Mainland of B.C., southern Ontario, and southern Alberta—outside the city, but close to city amenities and services.

As the Boomers begin to retire around 2015, a premium will also be placed on "age-proofed" housing, which makes independent retirement living a lot easier. This will include features like few, if any stairs; lots of light to assist older eyes; bathroom handles and railings; telephone and data jacks everywhere; voice-activated home-management software to control lights, the security system, and appliances; always-on broadband Internet connectivity; greater use of open space; fewer walls; wider doorways to accommodate mobility devices; contrasting colours to highlight surface changes; and levers instead of doorknobs.

- **Cottage and recreational property**. Driven by demographics and the increased availability of financing, cottages, hobby farms, ski chalets, and waterfront timeshares will remain good investments, especially those prime properties in demand areas.

  Don't expect every shack on every lake to rise in value, but the quality properties will—those which are all-season, on some water, on a paved road, and with lots of privacy, yet close to a town or major arterial road. Expect the boom in this kind of property, which has recently driven prices dramatically higher, to continue strongly, and for at least a decade.

- **Apartments**. This is the only kind of residential property I would buy for investment purposes—not a house, duplex, or condo high-rise unit, but, ideally, a small and manageable apartment building with a dozen to thirty units in it.

The collapse in mortgage rates has suddenly made the economics of these kinds of buildings make sense, because you can buy one with a relatively small down payment and be in positive cash flow from the start (something many condominium investors will soon find is impossible to do on a rental basis). In addition, a multi-unit residential building can give you income and tax options. The owner collects rent, which is considered eligible income for calculating RRSP contributions. When the building is sold, the profit can be taken as lightly taxed capital gains; or, as equity builds up over time, the place can be remortgaged, and the money removed free of any tax.

There is always a demand for rental housing in busy urban areas. Make sure to pick a building in a good location, and hire a property management company to run it.

Putting your mortgage in your RRSP

Yes, you can actually put a mortgage on your home inside your RRSP, which means you end up making monthly mortgage payments to yourself. It's a pretty cool idea, and many people have taken the considerable effort required to set it up. Now, why would you want to do this?

Simply because many people will need an income stream in their retirement, and yet they are reluctant to put their retirement funds in the stock market or mutual funds. By setting up an RRSP mortgage, they can enjoy a good rate of interest on their invested capital, and have the security that their own home is the asset underlying the whole deal, not some wild-eyed executive at a fibre optics company.

Working with a self-directed RRSP and the equity you've already built up in your home, you can transfer that equity to a tax-sheltered retirement plan. In fact, an RRSP mortgage will actually allow you to exceed the normal RRSP contribution limits. Now this strategy will only work if you have an amount of cash (or cashable investments) inside your RRSP equal to a mortgage currently in place on your home, or equal to one you will be placing upon it. It will cost a few thousand dollars to set up, and a few hundred a year in fees, but for many people it is a perfect homeowner's retirement solution.

Your RRSP is allowed to hold a mortgage on any Canadian real estate—either residential or commercial—that you own, or that is owned by an immediate relative. That means you can remove money from your RRSP and use it to lend as a mortgage; following which you must make regular payments back into your RRSP, just as you would with a bank mortgage.

For example, if you have a $100,000 mortgage in place on your home today, and $100,000 available inside your RRSP, then the retirement money can be used to pay off the bank loan. At that point, you have created a $100,000 RRSP mortgage, and will make regular payments to your retirement plan, rather than the bank.

Or, if your home is paid for now, you could simply borrow $100,000 against it on a home equity line of credit, and use the money to invest in, say, corporate bonds yielding a nice, conservative and stable rate of return in a non-registered portfolio. At the same time, take $100,000 from your RRSP and pay off the line of credit. At that point you would have accomplished several things:

- Established a $100,000 investment portfolio outside of your RRSP.

- Set up a $100,000 RRSP mortgage on your home, giving you the privilege of making monthly payments to your retirement plan. If the mortgage were established at 7%, then your monthly payment would be just over $700—a tax-free transfer of equity from your house into your RRSP.

- And you have, in effect, taken that $100,000 in cash that was inside your RRSP and invested it outside your plan without paying any tax. (Remember, you started with $100,000 and a paid-off house, and ended up owning a $100,000 mortgage in your RRSP and $100,000 worth of those corporate bonds outside your RRSP. In the course of this, you have created $100,000 in personal debt, payable to yourself over twenty-five years—the amortization of the mortgage. At $700 a month, you will actually contribute $210,000 to your RRSP over that period of time.)

So, given the peculiar nature of a mortgage, you end up paying yourself more than twice what you actually removed from your RRSP. Additionally, you can pay more into your RRSP on an annual basis than the contribution rules allow. That's because once you set up an RRSP mortgage, you must make regular monthly payments, regardless of what your annual income (the usual basis for determining contribution levels) might be.

And, of course, the money that accumulates inside your RRSP as you make mortgage payments to it can be used to invest in anything you want, such as more bonds or growth mutual funds. The idea here, however, is not to set this up in order to get a cheap mortgage on your house. Quite the opposite. The goal of an RRSP mortgage is to make it last as long as possible, and to be as costly as possible, so you can maximize the transfer of wealth into your tax-deferred retirement plan.

There are several ways of accomplishing this:

- Go with the longest amortization period possible, such as twenty-five years (but you can go longer). The more years it takes you to pay it off, the greater amount of interest money goes into the RRSP.

- The government stipulates that the rate of interest you determine for the RRSP mortgage must be comparable to market rates at the time it's set up. So, call around and find the highest possible rate being offered commercially, and use that for your RRSP mortgage.

- Make your RRSP mortgage an open one, giving you the privilege of paying it off at any time without penalty (which you will never do). Open mortgages come at a premium rate, which means the interest is greater.

- If you already have a mortgage in place on your home, you can create an RRSP mortgage as a second one, which boosts the interest rate even further. (But this will cost you more in mortgage insurance since all RRSP mortgages have to be insured either by GE Capital or CMHC.)

- Finally, don't use any of those techniques I wrote about earlier in this book for paying off your mortgage faster. This time, you want to pay it off slowly, incurring all the interest charges you can. So, go with a monthly-pay mortgage, instead of a weekly one.

An RRSP mortgage has the same flexibility and constraints as a bank mortgage: You can choose any length of term commercially available, and if you default on your payments, your RRSP mortgage ends up taking ownership of your house (which must then be sold off!). Your RRSP, according to the rules, can finance real estate, but it cannot own it.

Be aware that setting up an RRSP mortgage costs money and must be operated through a self-directed plan. You'll have to pay for a real estate appraisal and legal fees, and work with a financial institution, which will administer the mortgage. Also, as mentioned above, all RRSP mortgages must be insured, and the cost for that is an upfront fee equal to about 1.5% of the mortgage principal. Add that fee onto the mortgage amount, and have it amortized higher for payback.

Once in place, there will be some ongoing fees, such as the annual fee for the self-directed plan and an annual mortgage administration fee (because CCRA says you cannot be in charge of your own mortgage).

Some financial institutions will look at you funny when you say you're seeking an RRSP mortgage, and others will allow it only on your principal residence. Shop around. And remember, it's always best to work on this with the help of a financial adviser. I may be able to recommend one to you through garth.ca.

Real estate that pays you back

The vast majority of Canadians think nothing of plopping money down to buy a home, spending the next ten or fifteen years paying it off, and then sitting on the equity they built up for years, and years, and years. They are obviously content to have a roof over their heads and to wait for the ultimate cashing out, just as generations before have done.

But other people think that's nuts—a terrible use of money which could be working hard for you, instead of sitting dormant between the rafters. That's one reason many Canadians have taken out home equity loans, borrowing against the money they have accumulated in their houses to use for active purposes. Some people use the cash to renovate and add value to their homes, while others borrow to invest—in stocks, mutual funds, or investment real estate. In that case, when money is borrowed to make more money, all of the interest on a home equity loan is deductible from taxable income.

Investment real estate is property that has a cash flow attached to it, and there are many forms of it. Here are a few you might be considering:

- **A condo apartment unit**. This is the most common form of investment real estate and, in my mind, the worst. These days in cities like Toronto, Calgary, or Vancouver, it is virtually impossible for an investor to buy a half-decent downtown condo unit, and get enough rent out of it to cover municipal taxes and condo fees, even if the place is mortgage-free. That means the investor has tied up anywhere from $150,000 to $400,000 and is getting a zero rate of return.

  And while realtors will tell you that the tenant is paying

all the costs for you, there is absolutely no point buying the unit unless you can get a good capital gain on it in a relatively short period of time, like under five years. The trouble with the condo market is that when too many speculators move in, too many units get built, leading to years of stagnant prices. It happened in the late 1980s, and it may well be happening again as you read this.

- **A detached home.** Forget it. Same problems as with a single condo unit—it's very hard to make money and hard to sell a home that has been tenanted. Besides, being a landlord generally sucks.

- **A duplex, triplex, or four-plex**. This is a much better choice, since the economies of scale start clicking in. Many smart people have lived in one half of a duplex, while renting out the other for enough to carry the mortgage on the entire building. In general you will find property taxes on this kind of real estate to be quite reasonable, since most municipalities find they need to encourage rental housing. Mortgage lenders are also quite agreeable to financing these properties, since they have a predictable and steady cash flow. Investors in real estate with three or four dwelling units almost always make money, in good markets or bad.

- **An apartment building**. As discussed previously, owning an apartment building can make a ton of sense, and is a very vibrant and reasonable investment for anyone with a few hundred thousand dollars. For example, a three-storey building in Toronto with twenty-one units, worth $900,000, can be purchased with a down payment of around $135,000. The $765,000 mortgage, at 7%, carries for $5,358 a month, or $64,296 a year. After maintenance, utilities, and other overhead, the rent yields a positive cash flow of about

$25,000 a year—a very respectable 7% return on the $135,000 invested to buy the building.

The rental income qualifies as RRSP-eligible income for the owner, and the building can be remortgaged at any time, so the equity which has accumulated is removed, free of tax. You might also count on a good stream of quarters and loonies from the washing machines and dryers in the laundry room!

- **A commercial property**. This could be a plaza, restaurant, strip mall, industrial unit, car wash, or retail store. Once again, it all comes down to cash flow. Never buy a piece of commercial real estate unless it is generating money, and has stable, long-term tenants in it. Make any offer conditional upon an examination of the leases and a look at the books, as well as a complete physical inspection of the property. Also be very mindful of zoning bylaws and restrictions that could negatively affect the business, as well as any plans for major roadwork adjacent to it. Always, always, always use a professional real estate agent who specializes in commercial properties and who can help you find tenants in the future as required.

  I have owned stores and office space in the past. It was a thoroughly rewarding experience.

- **A business**. Sometimes a piece of property comes with an operating business attached to it. That means the cash flow generated by the business has to justify your investment in both the real estate and the corporation. The risk can be far greater, but so can the profits. Besides, operating a business is more involved, more intense, and a lot more interesting than just finding tenants to put into commercial space.

  If you are doing this, make sure to purchase the shares of the company which operates as a business and which also owns the property as a corporate asset. In that case, you'll pay a lot more in legal fees to execute a complicated share transfer, but you will avoid land transfer taxes on the real estate itself, for a huge net saving.

In addition, the vendor will be able to claim the $500,000 small business capital gains tax exemption, meaning no tax on that amount. This means, of course, you can beat him or her down further on the purchase price.

- **Real Estate Income Trusts (REITs).** This is a passive way to play the commercial, or income-producing, real estate game. There are all kinds of REITs available, from ones that own chains of hotels to trusts that aggregate residential apartment buildings in major centres. Some own only commercial office buildings, while others specialize in shopping malls. REITs have provided some excellent gains to investors in recent years, and can also pay you a regular stream of income.

  It's always a good idea to deal with a registered financial adviser when choosing any income trust.

The renovation revolution

The bustling residential real estate market that developed in earnest after September 11 has shaken the entire housing industry, from builders to real estate agents and brokers, and all of the trades: drywallers, plumbers, framers, electricians, carpenters, and those all-important backhoe operators.

From 1998 to 2001, housing starts roared ahead more than 20%, with a further jump of 23% in the first half of 2002. House prices, in a year when the stock market slumped by 20%, have risen by 7%. There is now a massive amount of money being diverted from financial assets into housing, whether that is ultimately wise or not. Billions more are being borrowed by people who are plunging into not only home buying but also home renovating.

In the first three months of 2002 alone, Statistics Canada recorded more than $18 billion in renovations, an 8% jump from 2000, with most of the action still to come. Most reno booms come six to twelve months after sales booms, which means that 2003 should be some of the best times in history for the guys who swing the hammers and lay the floor tiles.

Currently, one in every three Canadian homeowners is planning a renovation. This orgy of home improvements is being fuelled by consumer confidence, a big jump in job creation, a newfound love affair with real estate, and some of the lowest borrowing rates in history.

How best to finance a renovation?

The best way, naturally, is with that pile of cash sitting around in your chequing account earning 0.25% a year. If you don't have cash, then do not dip into your RRSP to renovate the house—that is meant to be long-term investment capital, and you will thank me when you're sixty-five.

The easiest and cheapest source of funds these days is a

home equity loan. You can borrow more than enough money, using your home as collateral. That means the loan is secured, and you will be offered the cash at the prime rate, which, as I write this, is a fantastic 4.5%. You can also arrange to make interest-only payments, although since the interest on an equity loan used for renovations is not tax-deductible, I'd suggest you pay it back just as quickly as possible.

Also be aware that interest rates will quite possible be higher in a year's time, so this is a good moment to strike and borrow for that major renovation.

How much lead time do I need?

As much as humanly possible is best, because the trades and all general contractors are exceptionally busy coping with a torrent of new work. The first step is to have plans drawn up, preferably by an architect, and then to get as many competing quotes as you can. Odds are there will be a huge variance between the quotes, so always make sure to get references on the short list of candidates.

Ask the contractor if he has adequate builder's insurance (in case your house burns down in the process), and make sure his workers are part of the provincial workplace safety insurance program. Get a precise quotation, clearly spelling out the scope of the work and the date on which it will be started and completed. Be suspicious of anyone who asks to be paid in cash, because chances are that they are operating as part of the underground economy. It may appeal to you to be a tax rebel and shaft the feds, but be aware that a contractor not paying taxes is probably not paying insurance premiums, either.

What permissions are required?

It depends on where your property is located, but you will certainly need a municipal building permit for additions to the house or major alterations of the exterior—even decks and porches. Landscaping generally does not require permission,

Homeowners, take a number

By Sahm Adrangi

Looking to fix up your house? Better luck next year. With over a third of homeowners planning a renovation, don't bet on finding a cheap, reliable contractor anytime soon. Just look at Derrick Francis and Deirdre Panet, a Toronto couple who are adding a new master bedroom, front veranda and step-down kitchen.

"It was brutal, just brutal trying to find someone," said Ms. Panet, a 38-year-old design consultant. "They were so busy they didn't need our business."

The couple finally found Peter Hillar at Greyfield Construction Company Ltd., but it took them dozens of phone calls, a slew of overpriced bids, and six weeks of searching. And of course, they've settled for a higher price than they first expected. With the summer's booming demand, forget about pinching your pennies.

"Quite honestly, we had enough trouble getting people to return prices for us," said Ms. Francis. "But when they did, they'd quote something off the top of their heads without even looking at any drawings — you know, just to see if we'd bite."

"One guy told me it was going to be $12,000 to excavate the backyard," added Mr. Francis, 42. "With the contractor we've got now, it's $3,800."

And sadly for consumers, the boiling demand has shown few signs of simmering. The reno market is closely linked to housing sales. When more consumers are buying houses, more are also renovating — many revampings occur right before a family moves into a new house. And Canadians have certainly been buying houses. Housing starts have surged 18% from 1998 to 2001, and resales of existing homes are up 21%. According to seasonally-adjusted figures, 23% more houses have changed hands in the first half of this year, compared with January to June, 2001.

As would be expected, renovations are also up. In the first quarter, Statistics Canada recorded $18.04-billion in home "alterations and improvements" — a 3.7% rise from last year and 8% higher than 2000. But there's a lag between housing booms and the home improvement market: A surging resale market today will mean a barrage of new renovations tomorrow. In fact, a recent Harvard study showed that new homebuyers spend about twice as much on improving a house as do current homeowners. First-time buyers spend about $2,900 annually; move-up buyers about $3,900.

> *'It was brutal, just brutal'*

See RENOVATION on Page IN4

The renovation industry has never been busier, as a result of the recent housing surge. A good rule of thumb is to never undergo a major renovation unless you are planning on staying in that home for five years. *Source: National Post* nor does shingling the roof or painting the exterior. Usually your contractor will get the necessary permissions for you.

In some places, all kinds of governmental bodies can be involved in a renovation. For example, a commercial property I own in Ontario is subject to the scrutiny of not only the local municipal and regional governments, but also the area conservation authority and a provincial body that oversees all land use. In this area people sometimes need permission to paint their shutters.

What renovations will add value to my home?

You can spend smart renovation money and stupid renovation money. Far and away, the best return for the money invested comes from painting. A new coat of paint can add thousands of dollars to the resale value of a home, both inside and out.

After that comes far more expensive renovations, but ones which are guaranteed to at least get your money back (within reason), like improving a kitchen or a bathroom. Turning a basement into a recreation or family room can be a good idea, especially in a bungalow, but be aware that subterranean living is not in vogue much these days. And a hard floor—tile or hardwood, replacing broadloom—is another winner.

On the stupid side, nothing comes close to a swimming pool for wasted money. This is not a cheap home improvement, but you will likely get little if anything back for making the investment. Many people consider pools to be an expensive accessory, of little value in a country which can have a brutally short, bug-infested, humidity-drenched summer. You are much better off, from a financial point of view, putting that cash into a Jacuzzi, or even a hot tub and a snazzy deck.

Building equity

Few Canadians would ever dream of buying stocks or mutual funds and borrowing 95% of the money required. That would be enough leverage to curl the toes of any financial adviser. But, when it comes to real estate, lots of young couples don't give that kind of borrowing a second thought. They plunk 5% of the purchase price down, borrow the other 95%, and even take the payment for the required mortgage insurance and add that onto their pile of debt.

They happily sign up for a mortgage that will not be paid off until twenty-five years later, and on which the early payments are more than 90% interest and just 10% or less repayment. Five years and sixty monthly payments later, they will owe just about exactly what they first borrowed. But they keep lining up to do this, because their parents and their parents before them did exactly the same—with one exception. One generation ago it was impossible to buy a home without at least 25% of the purchase price in cash, and a generation before that, you required at least half in cash.

In other words, the average Canadian home buyer has never been as indebted as today. This 95% financing has allowed lots of renters to turn into homeowners, but it has also taken many young and relatively financially free couples and turned them into massive debtors. Should the economy sour over the next decade; should interest rates spike higher; should the aging population poison the real estate market; should deflation actually drop housing prices—then these folks could see the value of their homes drop below the amount of debt they owe on them.

It's happened before, of course. Twenty years ago you could buy some perfectly nice houses in Alberta for a dollar, because their owners were desperate to unload homes worth less than the mortgages they had placed on them. In the greatest period of deflation yet experienced, in the 1930s—the period that followed the technology-driven stock market bubble of the 1920s—whole neighbourhoods of houses in Toronto went vacant, as banks foreclosed on mortgage defaults.

I am hardly suggesting a return to the Dirty Thirties, but I can easily envision a deflationary time over the next fifteen or twenty years as the economy is suddenly burdened with nine million new seniors—the greatest wave of retirees ever. For those people with 5% equity and 95% debt, that could be a nightmare scenario. The very possibility of it is a powerful reason to use every tool at your disposal to turn debt into equity.

Of course, this makes sense no matter what lies ahead. The capital gains you make on real estate, for example, are tax-free if they come from your principal residence. To make money—buying a home and hopefully selling it later for more than you paid—you need to reduce your debt load and increase your equity. Certainly, in the first half of your life, when real estate is the holy grail for most couples, the object is to build equity, but without becoming a slave to your mortgage. Remember, the days when inflation just naturally boosted the value of your home and made paying off a mortgage easier are gone, maybe forever—certainly for the next generation. So, take advantage of today's flexible and generous new mortgage rules that make building equity a lot easier. Here are some points to remember:

- **Go variable**. With a variable-rate mortgage, you will pay a far lower rate than with a fixed term, saving you lots of money, which can be applied as lump sum payments or increased monthly payments, against the mortgage principal. We are in a stable and low interest rate environment which could last for a number of years, so there is little need to lock in.

- **Go below prime**. All of the major lenders in this incredibly competitive environment offer a below-prime type product.

Typically, you get a big discount off the prime rate in the early months of the mortgage, then a smaller discount over the term of the next three years or so.

- **Go weekly**. Remember that by making fifty-two weekly payments a year rather than twelve monthly ones, you will pay off the mortgage years sooner and save a mountain of interest money. This is because you'll make the equivalent of an extra monthly payment per year, plus reduce compound interest costs. Also check out the Manulife One account, which automatically makes a mortgage payment every time you receive a pay cheque.

- **Max out the down payment**. Yes, you can borrow 95% of the cost of the house, but the more down payment you can cough up, the more equity you will have, and the easier the debt will be to repay. There are now mainstream lenders introducing 100% financing for homeowners with lots of cash flow but little in the way of savings. This is like renting a house but still being responsible for buying it.

- **Get pre-approved**. This way you will know, based on your income and down payment, exactly how much debt you can actually handle. Your mortgage interest rate will be locked in, giving you protection against any increases while allowing you to enjoy any decreases. Your hand will be strengthened when you come to make an offer, because it will not be conditional upon financing. Pre-approval is fast, simple, and free.

- **Shop around**. The mortgage business is incredibly competitive, dominated by the major banks. A mortgage is considered a "relationship" product, which means the lender of your home loan will probably end up with your car loan, RRSP, and mutual funds. That's why the competition is keen, and the deals great. Shop around, finding the best terms and the deepest discount off posted rates.

- **Use pre-payment tools**. As mentioned in "Finding the perfect mortgage, Part II," you have an arsenal of tools to allow for faster pre-payment of the principal. Use them aggressively. If you do not, making regular monthly payments for the term of your mortgage, you will end up paying back about three times the entire amount you borrowed—not good financial planning.

- **Forget the insurance**. The mortgage insurance offered you by your lender will be some of the most expensive on the planet. This should really only be a concern if you are ill, in a job with a high risk of being laid off, or have a young family and no other insurance. Otherwise, just go with regular term insurance, which you should have anyway. As well, try to avoid adding the costs of insurance on a high-ratio mortgage (more than 75% of the home's value) on to the principal. This costs a lot, and in many cases you're better off getting the money through a second mortgage or a line of credit.

- **Borrow again**. Build your equity, so you can start using it, by borrowing against it. For many Canadians, this is an ideal source of tax-deductible investment capital.

Using equity

Once you have built up equity inside your residential real estate, then you can start using it. As I mentioned previously, setting up a home equity loan is like using your home as a private bank. You can reach in and scoop up all those mortgage payments you made over the years, use the money to invest in something else, and get a whopping break on your personal income taxes by deducting all the loan interest.

This works best if you set up a loan with interest-only payments. And it only works if you use the cash to buy something that will pay you income, like stocks which pay dividends, or real estate that generates rent, or has the potential to pay you a capital gain, like common stocks, mutual funds, or corporate bonds. But, I hear you mutter, is it not a risky strategy to borrow against real estate (especially your home), to put the money into financial assets that could decline in value?

In 1995, when the TSE 300 was near the 5,000 mark, I started to suggest to people that the stock market would likely outperform real estate over the next ten years, and it would make a lot of sense for them to borrow against paid-off homes to buy mutual funds. Within five years, the TSE had doubled to 10,000, and the strategy looked brilliant. Two years later, with the TSE back down at 6,500, in the wake of September 11, WorldCom, Enron, and the technology meltdown, money poured back out of mutual funds and into real estate. In any case, and despite that temporary plunge, the five-year return was 30%. What can we expect next?

If history is any guide, and it should be, then stocks and mutual funds based upon them will continue to give the best return, as they have over the last five generations. If inflation in North America is likely to remain nonexistent, or very low, then so will interest rates. Low rates are positive for corporate profits and for the stock market, and negative for savers who cannot grow money fast enough in bonds or GICs. Meanwhile, the biggest generation in history—the Baby Boomers—is now entering its peak income-earning and spending years, which is very positive for economic growth and capital markets. This mass of people now has about fifteen years to pump up retirement savings, and the stock market, through diversified mutual funds, is the best place to accomplish that.

So as the turbulent early years of the new millennium unfold, with their shocking terrorist and accounting events coming on the heels of a stock market that frothed higher than anyone could have imagined, many people are confused. Blinded by current events, they have lost sight of the fundamentals that move markets. Only if you believe the economy will stop growing, that corporations will cease making money, and that technological advance will cease, should you abandon financial assets.

Real estate is a great core holding, and for many people will always form the cornerstone of personal financial planning, but it should also be viewed as a tool to help you acquire assets with a great track record of growth. As humans live longer and longer lives, the amount of cash required to get through thirty years of retirement grows exponentially. In an environment of low interest rates, getting it through "safe" investing in interest-bearing products like GICs or savings bonds is an impossibility. Like it or not, we should all be exposed to the capital markets through diversified mutual funds and with the help of a professional financial adviser. And you should seriously consider using your personal bank—i.e., your home—to finance this.

A home equity loan is not like a mortgage, because you control how big it is. Set up an equity loan for $100,000, for example, but just draw down the amount you want, and when you need it. Typically the money would just flow into your bank account after you wrote a cheque to buy financial assets.

And you can pay down a line of credit at any time, without

penalty, unlike most mortgages. But there is a powerful argument against paying it off once set up, and that's the deductibility of all interest. If you get an equity loan with interest-only payments, then the lump sum of all the interest you pay each year can be deducted from the taxable income you earn working for a living. That means for most middle-class Canadians in the top tax bracket, that 50% of the loan interest comes right off the tax you send to Ottawa.

Home equity loans are secured debt, which means the real estate stands behind it. As such, you will get the money at the lowest possible rate: prime. So, if the prime rate is 5%, then the effective after-tax cost of the equity loan is half that, or 2.5%. Should you expect your financial assets to beat that? You bet, especially if you use a professional adviser to assist you.

For example, I give my investment money to a discretionary portfolio manager, which means I don't even know what he buys and sells. But it works. In 2002, when the markets took a 30% dive, my portfolio earned a positive return of 7%. My portfolio manager was smart enough to spot winning companies and dump losers, which is exactly what smart mutual fund managers do.

Because the debt of a home equity loan is secured, and considered to be safe, you can borrow up to 75% of the appraised value of your home, however I would counsel against that level of debt. Markets do go up and down in a volatile fashion, and if you borrow a lot, you might have trouble sleeping at night, panic, and take your money out after an asset has declined. That locks in a loss, which no long-term investor should ever do.

But it happens all the time. For example, in the summer of 2002, when the TSX was at its lowest point in more than forty months, Canadian mutual fund investors cashed in more than $2.2 billion worth of funds in just a two-month period. They panicked and sold at the market's low, just as many had plowed money into Nortel and science and technology funds in 2000, when the market peaked.

This is why anyone borrowing money to invest, which is a fundamentally sound strategy, should always remember the three sacred rules:

1) **Be there for the long term**—not five months, but five years.
2) **Be diversified**. Invest in a basket of stocks or a diversified equity fund, not a single company or two.
3) **Be well advised**. Investing in financial assets is more complicated than fixing your computer. Do you really want an amateur looking after your money? Then stop doing it.

The most social of assets

Real estate is addictive, and I have been smitten many times. That's because it is a human, social asset, not created by nature, but built by hand. Buying a piece of property is completely unlike buying a stock or a mutual fund, because it has form, texture, and history. It's different from other physical assets, like a piece of gold or a new motorcycle, because it cannot be moved.

Real estate helps to define its owner, saying much about his or her wealth, tastes, social status, and lifestyle. You can often tell as much from the size, style, design, and location of a house as from the biography of the person who bought it, or had it built. An important part of everyone's background and current station in life is the neighbourhood or place they came from, or have travelled to.

So, real estate is intensely local in its nature. A property is worth what it's worth for local reasons—the street, population mix, neighbouring stores, schools or factories, transportation routes, water, trees, air quality—as much as it is for economic ones, like mortgage rates, job creation, and migration. A local market evolves, controlled by the buyers and sellers in it, governed by the real estate infrastructure of agent, broker, and real estate board.

That is why buying and selling a property is so unique, and so organic. It's not like buying a stock, whose value is determined by thousands or millions of people and published daily. Real estate values can change overnight, as the balance between buyers and sellers changes. But this is also a hard asset, costing hundreds of thousands of dollars, and representing the single greatest purchase that most people make in their entire lives.

Real estate has built fortunes and it has destroyed them. There is no constant with an asset that has no inherent value—only perceived value.

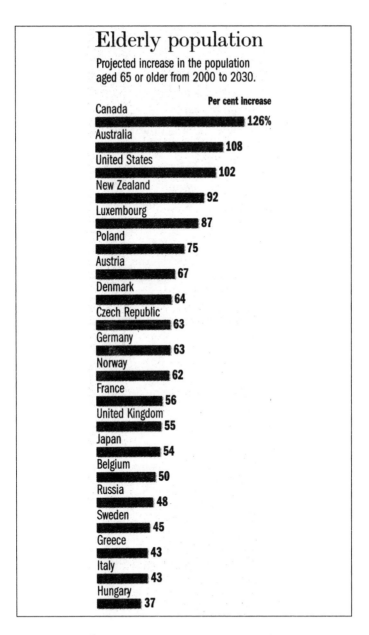

Elderly population

Projected increase in the population aged 65 or older from 2000 to 2030.

Per cent increase

Canada
126%

Australia
108

United States
102

New Zealand
92

Luxembourg
87

Poland
75

Austria
67

Denmark
64

Czech Republic
63

Germany
63

Norway
62

France
56

United Kingdom
55

Japan
54

Belgium
50

Russia
48

Sweden
45

Greece
43

Italy
43

Hungary
37

Changing demographics will have a profound impact on residential real estate as Canada leads the world with an aging population. Beware the influence of geriatric Boomers! *Source: Toronto Star*

So, as I have argued in this little book about the subject, you should always strive to buy real estate that will have the best shot at appreciating, for all of the vague reasons mentioned. Going forward, one of the most profound influences on the market will be the aging of the Canadian population, which will translate into rapidly shifting housing needs and tastes.

Today, on average, a seventy-year-old man can expect to live for another seventeen years. Even more remarkable, a seventy-four-year-old woman today will likely live twenty-one more years. As the decade unfolds, those numbers will increase. We are probably less than a generation away from an average life span of 100 years.

Over the next twenty years, the number of retired Canadians will double, to almost nine million, two million less than the number of young people who will enter the work-force. Between 2000 and 2030, the number of Canadians over age sixty-five will increase by 126%, compared with 102% in the U.S. and 55% in Britain.

The implications are clear for the public pension and health care systems—it could end up being a disaster. But when it comes to real estate, far less thought appears to be devoted to the subject of our changing country. There are a lot of fifty-year-olds today, and the majority of them own a home which may be appropriate for someone their age, but not for when they hit seventy, seventy-five, or eighty. Who will they sell to, and when? Will many houses hit the market at roughly the same time to swamp demand and depress prices?

Will we have new millions of people who will want to live in urban areas, with lots of services, in housing that is maintenance-free? Will there be government programs subsidizing seniors to live independently, in their own homes, as an alternative to incredibly expensive institutional housing?

Does that mean a new renaissance for urban bungalows and condominium townhomes and apartments, and an inevitable decline of the suburbs, where life is impossible without a car?

If real estate takes a demographic hit fifteen years from now, will banks and other lenders feel the same way about it, giving you 95% financing, or loans at prime against your equity? Probably not, which could make this an absolutely unique time for real estate investors and owners in the sweep of modern history.

The lessons may be obvious: Lofts are a questionable investment, while one-storey city houses are a great one. Multi-bedroom homes in distant suburbs will face a smaller and smaller number of buyers, while condos of all kinds will continue to find wide appeal. And the supply of homes for sale over the next fifteen years is far more likely to rise than fall. After all, most of those fifty-year-old Boomers are house-rich and investment-asset-poor. For millions of them, turning real estate into retirement cash is the only reasonable option they have, unless they want to work well into their seventies and eighties.

So, real estate does have a future, but it will be unlike the one your parents or grandparents expected. This most social of assets will rise and fall with the times, which are becoming more volatile, and yet extremely predictable. You need somewhere to live, for sure. You can make money in real estate, without a doubt. But today, more than ever, you need real estate wisdom.

garth.ca

Take another five minutes and go on-line to **garth.ca**. I'm a huge believer in the Internet and its ability to contain, organize and present information. This is a medium that will turn out to be more powerful than radio, television and the telephone combined. In fact, over time, it will come to absorb those technologies, causing nothing short of a revolution in human communication.

At **garth.ca** you will find daily updates on the markets and personal finance strategies, and a large, searchable base of archived information. There is also a live video feed direct from the broadcast centre of Millennium Media Television, the company of which I am chief executive officer.

Other features of special interest to readers of this book:

A weekly update
Every Sunday there is an update to this book published on-line at **garth.ca**, in the "columns" area. Please take five minutes on Sunday evening or during the week to read it. This is material I personally research and write, and it is yours to benefit from, free of charge.

A video version
Watch a video version of this book on-line. If you have been unable to attend one of my live seminars, or would like to view the latest update, here is an opportunity. The video can be watched in streaming media, downloaded or ordered—burned on a CD or in VHS format for a small charge.

The Turner Report
Ten times a year I produce an in-depth newsletter, published on the fifteenth of the month, featuring mutual fund picks, stocks to watch, tax and investment strategies, and a national

panel of top financial advisers who provide complete answers to subscribers' questions. Delivered by letter mail or e-mail, *The Turner Report* is available for a small monthly fee and offers a 100% money-back guarantee. You will find more information and a free sample on-line.

If you need to reach me, here's how:

By mail: Garth Turner
                    372 Bay Street, Suite 600
                    Toronto, Ontario M5H 2W9
                    Fax: (416) 489-2189

To book a seminar: Gisele Robert
                    Speaker Solutions
                    (416) 489-2188
                    1-877-489-2188 toll-free

On-line: (personal)   garth@garth.ca
          (corporate)   garth@MillenniumMedia.tv

Index

(see above)